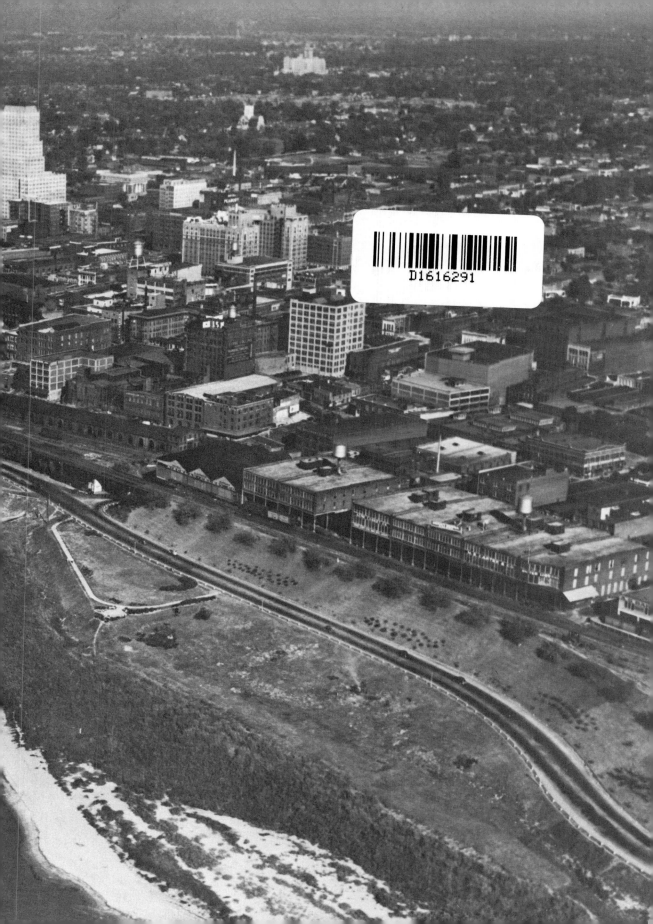

Yesterday's Memphis

Seemann's Historic Cities Series

CHARLES W. CRAWFORD

Yesterday's
MEMPHIS

Seemann's Historic Cities Series No. 25

E. A. Seemann Publishing, Inc.
Miami, Florida

Many individuals and institutions supported the author's task of collecting photographs for this book. Their contributions are gratefully credited in abbreviated form at the end of each caption; all pictures without credit are from the author's collection. The contributors are the following:

BC	Becky Crouch Collection, Memphis	Martin	Frances Duffy Martin, Memphis
Bobbit	Charles A. Bobbitt, Memphis	MATA	Memphis Area Transit Authority
BP	Bert Prosterman Collection, Memphis	MM	Memphis Museum
BW	Bobby Williams Collection, Memphis	MPL	Memphis Public Library
CA	*Commercial Appeal*, Memphis	MSU	Memphis State University
C of C	Memphis Area Chamber of Commerce	Polk	Margaret Polk, Memphis
CJH	Charles J. Hooker, New York	Roper	Dr. James E. Roper, Memphis
CR	Mrs. Charles Rudy, Memphis	RRC	*The Robert R. Churches of Memphis,*
Cubbins	Marie Cubbins, Memphis		by Annette E. & Roberta Church
Dambrino	Peggy Dambrino, Memphis	Thompson	John Thompson Collection, Memphis
Dredge	John Dredge Collection, Memphis	TSLA	Tennessee State Library and Archives,
Evans	Henry Evans, Memphis		Nashville
Harper's	*Harper's Weekly,* New York	Wade	Bert Wade Collection, Memphis
HEG	Harry Goodwin Collection	Williams	Ed Williams, Memphis
McLemore	Mrs. D. W. McLemore, Memphis		
McWhorter	John McWhorter, Memphis		

Library of Congress Cataloging in Publication Data

Crawford, Charles Wann, 1931-
   Yesterday's Memphis.

   (Seemann's historic cities series ; no. 25)
   Includes index.
   1. Memphis--History--Pictorial works. 2. Memphis--
Description--Views. I. Title.
F444.M5C7   976.8'19   76-10384
ISBN 0-912458-69-0

Manufactured in the United States of America.

To
Robert L. Crawford and Charles R. Crawford,
associate editors, aides-de-camp, *sui generis,* my sons.

Contents

Preface

A MAJOR THEME in the history of the United States has been the steady growth of large urban centers from a society that was originally almost completely rural. In the South, even though the importance of agriculture has been strong and persistent, this theme has also been noticeable. Memphis, in part because it was established in a rich farming region, grew in less than half a century into the sixth largest city in the South and the most populous in its state. Despite the difficulties it has experienced, it has remained a leading city.

This book is an account of the development of the city that was built on the Fourth Chickasaw Bluff of the Mississippi River, from its beginning to the era of the Korean War. Making use of the written word, as well as historical photographs and other pictures, it undertakes to present the richly varied subjects of the city's life with as much professional accuracy as possible.

The value of a study such as this is greatly improved by the use of photographs. A historian hopes that his judgment will be sound enough and his selections wise enough that his portrait of the past will be true. But photographic evidence presents the past exactly as it appeared at the time without the limitations of human description and interpretation. All historical records, however, are incomplete, and collections of photographs are no exception. Prominent landmarks, successful people, and dramatic events were often recorded in pictures. Many people, as well as many groups of people, who have played parts in the history of the city have been as neglected in photographs as they have in the printed word. Moreover, many collections of photographs have been lost. To the regret of historians, they are gone like François Villon's snows of yesteryear.

Memphis is fortunate in having some of its historical records preserved and accessible to interested researchers. I wish to express special thanks to the Memphis Public Library and to its competent and helpful staff members: Dan Yanchisin, Steven Findlay, James Johnson, Benjamin Head, Josiah Brady, Katherine Embury, Joan Cannon, and Delanie Ross. They have the finest collection of photographs in the city. Important aid was also given by Thomas Rhodes and Brier Smith of the Memphis Museum.

The *Commercial Appeal,* which has made important contributions to Memphis history for many years, has provided useful information for his book. I am indebted to William Sorrels, Bob Williams, Lynn Stewart, Gene Brady, and George Dunn.

Aid and encouragement was given in the preparation of parts of the book by Brenda Meier, Harry Godwin, and Eleanor Hughes. Also, without the loyal support of Prof. Sam Proctor, of the University of Florida, this book would not have been written. Much information necessary for the written portions of the book came from the West Tennessee Historical Society and the Oral History Research Office of Memphis State University.

The last debt is greatest: Of the 623,530 people who are Memphis residents, the one who probably knows more about the history of the city than any other is Paul R. Coppock, retired newspaperman, historian, and respected friend. He provided answers to my questions about yesterday's Memphis when they could not be found elsewhere.

Charles W. Crawford

Memphis

From Wilderness
to Western Town

AT FIRST there was the land, shaped by the wind and the river. Together the wind and the water formed one of the more favorable sites for a city on the continent. Over a period of time, perhaps lasting several million years, the winds blowing across North America deposited vast amounts of loess soil, building it into a large mass near where the thirty-fifth parallel of north latitude crossed the greatest river of the continent. This river, flowing southward for twenty-five hundred miles to the Gulf of Mexico, moved with the weight of the water drained from 1,244,000 square miles of land. From the Appalachians to the Rockies it gathered water from innumerable small streams pouring into more than forty major tributary streams, which in turn flowed into the main trunk to make the Mississippi—monarch of North American rivers. Drawn toward the Gulf by the force of gravity, the Mississippi scoured a mighty channel through the loessial hills. The current eroded steep bluffs which stood high above the waters.

When men first entered the great river valley they were directed by nature to these eminences, for the Mississippi along almost all of its lower reaches had low and muddy banks which in flood seasons became extensive swamps. Where these high bluffs reached the river's edge, the earliest men found suitable living sites, and there later cities would appear: Baton Rouge, Vicksburg, Helena, and Memphis. For several thousand years, however, only the Indians made use of the bluffs, witnessing, mainly, the natural changes wrought by time and the elements, while their cultures endured through the stages later classified by scholars as Archaic, Woodland, and Mississippian.

On the other side of the planet during these years, the pyramids were built, Rome flourished and fell, Christianity and Islam were established, the Renaissance passed, and Columbus crossed the Atlantic. Then, the slow pace of life on the Chickasaw bluffs neared its greatest change, as European exploration of the Americas began.

In 1541, Hernando De Soto and his army crossed the Mississippi River at a site near the lower bluff, the first Europeans to see the lower half of the great river. De Soto died nearby, and was reportedly buried in the river so that hostile Indians would not dig up his grave and despoil his remains.

More than one hundred years later, in 1673, white men again journeyed down the river. Two Frenchmen, Jacques Marquette, a missionary of the Jesuit order, and Louis Joliet (or Jolliet), a Quebec fur trader, went as far south as the mouth of the Arkansas River looking for a route to the Pacific Ocean. When they stopped at the Chickasaw Bluffs, they found to their surprise that the Chickasaw Indians living there had several items—guns, knives, and glass—that could be obtained only from white men or from Indians who traded with white men.

The first structure in the area was erected by order of Robert Cavalier, sieur de La Salle, another Frenchmen who followed Joliet and Marquette nine years later. While hunting on one of the upper bluffs, the armorer of La Salle's party, Pierre Prudhomme, was lost. During the search for him a rough palisade of logs was built for security against the Indians. Prudhomme was finally found, uninjured, drifting down the river on a make-shift raft. But his bad sense of direction had earned him a place in history, for the fort and bluffs were named after him. Although the fort was inhabited only once, the "Heights of Prudhomme" became the common name of the bluffs for many years.

After this time, the French were the dominating force on the river. Their trade up and down the river was hampered, however, by the small, warlike tribe of the Chickasaws. These Indians' hatred of the French was caused by two things: the French alliance with the Choctaws, ancestral enemies of the Chickasaws; and France's persistent intrusion into Chickasaw tribal ground. Aided by the British, the tribe continually warred on the French traders, often raining arrows down from the bluffs onto their boats. Three attempts by mixed forces of French and allied Indians to crush the Chickasaws were defeated by the fierce tribe—and by diseases, which were even more deadly than arrows. In the second of these campaigns, led by Jean Baptiste Lemoyne, sieur de Bienville, the founder of New Orleans, Fort Assumption was built on the present-day site of Memphis. The French and Indian War of 1754-1763, which ended with the cession of all land east of the Mississippi River to the British and of Louisiana to the Spanish, marked the close of the French presence on the bluffs.

Spain was the next nation to attempt to gain control there. The Chickasaws quickly switched their hostility to these new would-be conquerors, adopting the same policy toward them that they had employed so successfully against the French. American settlers in Middle Tennessee, though ostensibly allies of Spain, did not wish for the Spaniards to control the river, so they provided munitions and supplies for the Chickasaws.

In 1784, the Spanish concluded a treaty with the stubborn tribe, a treaty that began a "cold war" between the United States and Spain that was to last until the turn of the century. The Chickasaws divided into two factions: One, led by Chief Wolf's Friend, favored the Spanish; the other, led by Chief Piomingo, favored the American frontiersmen.

It was not until 1793, however, that any real endeavors were made by either side to acquire the bluffs. In that year, William Clark journeyed to the future site of Memphis to

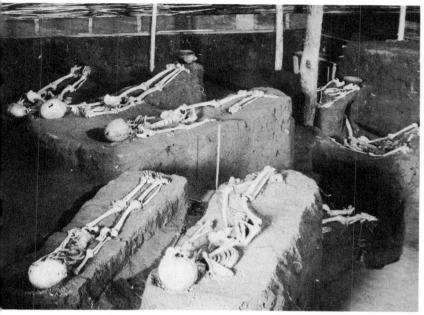

BURIALS AT CHUCALISSA, illustrated in these two photographs of excavated graves, often included burying tools, weapons, and pottery with the bodies. The skeletons and artifacts shown are now in one of the buildings at the village, displayed as they were when discovered. First used well before 1000 A. D., Chucalissa was abandoned during the 1500s. It is located about six miles south of the downtown area of Memphis.

EARLY INDIAN INHABITANTS of the Memphis area constructed their own dwellings and villages along the Mississippi River and the tributary streams flowing into it. Although all of these towns disappeared centuries ago, their sites can be located and mapped today. The villages can even be reconstructed much as they were when the Indians lived in them. Chucalissa, rebuilt with considerable accuracy, is seen in this aerial view.

[13]

gain the aid of Indians living there. In 1794, John Overton, a man who was destined to figure prominently in the future history of Memphis, purchased a piece of land on the bluff.

This and other instances of American interest in the area, such as the Georgia sale of land in West Tennessee and reports of Americans at Muscle Shoals on the Tennessee River, prompted Don Manuel de Lemos Gayoso, governor of Louisiana, to hurry his plans for a fort on the lower bluff. Just over two weeks later, on May 31, the Spanish flag was raised over Fort San Fernando de las Barrancas.

The United States, alarmed by this intrusion upon its territory, sent Capt. Joseph Guion to warn the Spanish that their move was considered hostile. By the time that Guion arrived at the bluffs, however, the Spanish had withdrawn to the western bank of the Mississippi River and built Fort Esperanza. A short time later, they abandoned this post also. Captain Guion, after getting a tract of land from the allied Chickasaw chief, Piomingo, built Fort Adams. It was later replaced by Fort Pickering, named after the then secretary of state, Timothy Pickering.

Between the years 1797, when Fort Pickering was built, and 1819, when Memphis was laid out, little of note occurred on the bluff. A prolonged visit by the noted French novelist, Volney, to a settlement on the west bank, and a time during which Zachary Taylor, the future president, was commander at Fort Pickering were two of the few notable events. Besides the soldiers in the garrison, only a handful of white men lived there, most of them involved in trade with the Indians, who were still the most numerous

INDIAN STICK BALL, a demanding and sometimes violent game, is still played at Chucalissa by Indians living in the area. These players are mainly Choctaws. The original name of the village is unknown. *Chucalissa* is a word meaning "abandoned town" in the Choctaw language. Managed by Memphis State University, the village is open to the public.

group around. Despite this stagnation, a few far-sighted men saw the potential for a large, successful city on the lower bluff.

John Overton was one of these men. On May 1, 1819, he and his partners, Andrew Jackson and James Winchester, laid out the town of Memphis on a five-thousand-acre tract of bluff land that they had purchased in 1794 from the brother of the original owner, John Rice, who had been killed by Indians. Rice had originally bought the land from the State of North Carolina in 1783. The acreage, which included a strategic landing site at Wolf River, was destined to become the heart of present-day Memphis.

Through his influence in Nashville, Overton caused Shelby County to be formed in November, only five months after Memphis was surveyed. He then began to publicize the investment through the newspapers of several large cities, such as New Orleans and St. Louis. Even with this measure, land sales were slow. Jackson soon traded his piece of the land to John C. McLemore because of problems with squatters which he felt would damage his 1824 presidential platform as the champion of the common man.

Isaac Rawlings, who had been on the bluff since 1813, was one of the first merchants, and a proprietor of a store for many years, until he was forced out of business by his rival, Marcus Winchester. Rawlings was also a magistrate, served five times as mayor, and ran for the post of delegate to the 1834 Tennessee Constitutional Convention as an opponent of slavery. In 1840, just before his death, he had himself carried in a chair so that he could go to vote for the Whig ticket.

Marcus Winchester, a sophisticated and learned man, was also an important figure on the bluff during the early days of Memphis. His financial skills and intelligence made him a success. His store replaced Rawlings' as the most popular place to trade soon after it was opened. His marriage to a woman of partially black descent, however, almost ruined him in Memphis. Although many men, including Rawlings, lived with their housekeepers, it was not considered proper to marry outside of one's race. The criticism that Winchester received drove him to drink, and cut short his career.

Most of the trade done in Memphis at this time, besides that with steamboats, was with flatboatmen. These were ordinary farmers who loaded their goods, anything they had grown or made, onto rectangular box-shaped craft and floated them down the nearest stream to the Mississippi (or the Tennessee or the Cumberland) to a town where they could sell or trade their wares.

As more and more people moved into the area, cotton became the major crop. Throughout the 1820s and 1830s, however, Memphis was not blessed with trade in the burgeoning cotton market, because of several outbreaks of disease, including yellow fever, which was to devastate the lower bluff half a century later. The city was soon thought of as unhealthy, and this unsavory reputation helped to divert trade from it to Randolph, a town several miles north on another of the Chickasaw Bluffs.

The financial crisis of 1837 started the move of trade toward Memphis and, by 1838, low water had forced steamboats to move their business from Randolph to Memphis, further insuring the dominance of the latter. The opening of the Mississippi Territory to settlement was another major factor in this important development.

But the lower-bluff city's victory over its northern counterpart, although financially

JOHN OVERTON, a Nashville businessman who was one of the wealthiest men in Tennessee, became the first proprietor of Memphis in 1794 when he bought the five-thousand-acre tract of land on the Fourth Chickasaw Bluff that North Carolina had conveyed to John Rice in 1783. Rice was killed by Indians, and Overton bought the land from the heirs for five hundred dollars. It was located on the river bank north of present Union Avenue and west of East Parkway. When the city was laid out, Overton still owned one-half of the tract. (TSLA)

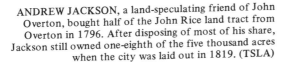

ANDREW JACKSON, a land-speculating friend of John Overton, bought half of the John Rice land tract from Overton in 1796. After disposing of most of his share, Jackson still owned one-eighth of the five thousand acres when the city was laid out in 1819. (TSLA)

JAMES WINCHESTER, a Middle Tennessee landowner, bought an interest in the John Rice tract from the one-half held by Andrew Jackson. In 1819, Winchester held a one-fourth interest, and the heirs of his brother, William Winchester, owned one-eighth. (TSLA)

satisfying, did not mark any improvements in its physical aspects. If anything, the influx of large numbers of people made Memphis an even less desirable place to live. Human and animal waste cluttered the streets and alleys, and sanitation was such a problem that some travelers said that the smell was the most memorable part of their visit. The streets were so full of deep holes that filled with water when the frequent rains came that one account of this tells of a team of oxen that drowned.

Entertainment at this time included dueling (the spectators, not the duelists, were the ones entertained), dancing, and camp meetings. Camp meetings were the most popular because they gave an excuse for many activities from drinking to courting. Although the sermons were long, they were sometimes mercifully difficult to hear. There were invariably those who "heard the word of the Lord" and engaged in energetic body contortions and loud shouting and screaming. An area padded with hay was often provided for these affected people so they would not hurt themselves as they rolled and shouted in religious ecstasy.

As Memphis continued to grow, more sophisticated entertainments appeared, and minstrel shows, circuses, and showboats were included. By 1842, Memphis even had the City Theatre, a rather amateurish attempt at play-acting. The plays were performed in a stable, which fact, according to Gerald Capers, encouraged some remarks about the quality of acting. But for a town where bears had roamed through the streets only a few years before, it was a good beginning.

The flatboatmen who had provided much of early Memphis' commerce were also one of her greatest nemeses. These men, usually ordinary and law-abiding citizens in their home towns, treated their flatboat trips much as modern-day businessmen do conventions. For years they terrorized the citizens, insulting and physically abusing them, and they refused to pay the wharfage fee that would have allowed the city to improve itself. In 1842, under the leadership of Mayor William Spickernagle, the Memphis wharfmaster attempted to collect the tax from a group of about five hundred flatboats that had tied up at the town. He was chased back up the bluff, but returned with the constable and a warrant. These two were promptly run back into town. When they returned with a number of militiamen, a fight ensued in which one of the more pugnacious flatboatmen was killed and the others were forced to pay the tax. This event marked the beginning of Memphis as an independent, powerful city.

After asserting control over the flatboatmen, Memphis began a pattern of growth that made it one of the largest Southern cities on the eve of the Civil War. The town, which had a population of only 1,799 in 1850, grew to a population of 22,623 by 1860. The most important factor in this dramatic increase in size was the rise in the importance of cotton.

Eli Whitney's invention of the cotton gin made profitable the opening of land in Mississippi, Alabama, Arkansas, and Texas to large-scale cotton growing. Memphis, ideally located as a shipping center and supply depot for West Tennessee, Northern Alabama, Arkansas, and Northern Mississippi, grew with the cotton trade. For example, in 1840 Memphis dealers handled 35,000 bales of cotton, worth $3,000,000. By the mid-1850s,

JOHN C. McLEMORE, a friend of Andrew Jackson, took Old Hickory's place as the third proprietor of Memphis, Jackson, who was preparing for his presidential campaign in 1824, transferred his one-eighth interest to McLemore, who came to the city and became one of its most active promoters. He was a supporter of the La Grange and Memphis Railroad and other enterprises. Buried at Elmwood Cemetery, he was the only one of the Memphis proprietors to be interred in the city they founded. His descendants have been active in business in Memphis to the present. (McLemore)

Memphis was America's largest inland cotton market. In 1860, Memphis dealers handled 360,653 bales, worth $18,500,000.

Influenced to a large degree by the growing importance of cotton and the need to transport it from the outlying areas to Memphis, the quality and quantity of the city's transportation system also grew. A plan to improve roads, usually by replacing the original dirt with more dirt, was started in the 1830s. A scheme in the early 1850s to upgrade the routes to such towns as La Grange, Germantown, Somerville, Horn Lake, and Hernando by planking the roads met with only limited success.

Railroads played a vital role in the growth and development of Memphis, serving not only to link cotton plantations to the city, but also tying Memphis to other cities of the South and of the nation. In the early 1840s, the Memphis and La Grange, a short-lived local route, carried citizens to a point then about six miles away, the area now known as White Station. The Memphians would detrain, eat a picnic lunch, then return to Memphis.

The Memphis and Charleston Railroad, chartered in 1846, was the first railroad connecting Memphis with another major city, but troubled by litigation from the towns it had by-passed, it grew slowly. It was August of 1852 before it reached Germantown, and was not completed until March 28, 1857. This occasion was noted by numerous celebrations, including one in Memphis during which a fire engine from Charleston pumped water into the Mississippi, symbolizing the linking of the Atlantic Ocean to the Mississippi.

Following the formation of the Memphis and Charleston, three other rail lines were begun from Memphis. The Memphis and Ohio, linking the city with Louisville and Cincinnati, was begun in the late 1850s. The Mississippi and Tennessee, chartered in 1852, connected Memphis by rail with New Orleans. And the Memphis and Little Rock, though not finished until the 1870s, was begun in the early 1860s.

Before the middle of the century, steamboats began to play a major role on the Mississippi. Able to travel both up and down river at a relatively swift speed, the steamers added a new dimension to trade and communication. During the 1850s, steamboat lines ran from Memphis to New Orleans, St. Louis, Louisville, and Cincinnati, as well as to smaller towns such as Little Rock and Vicksburg. In addition to their popularity as a luxurious means of travel, they soon played a significant role in the transportation of cotton along the length of the Mississippi River system.

Ante-bellum Memphis also gave thought to the development of industry, in an attempt to change its deserved reputation as a one-product (cotton) town. The 1840s therefore saw the beginnings of small businesses such as William Strebbling's carriage production and W.A. Bickford's building-supply firm. In addition to two flour mills and two machine works, by 1850 the city also manufactured finer goods such as pianos—with bricks, tinware, boots, carriages, steam engines, soap, mineral water, and hats and caps only some of its other products. By 1860 Memphis had an industrial output valued at about four million dollars.

The growing transportation system that eased the shipment of cotton also increased the importance of Memphis as a distribution center for the area. The first wholesale grocery in the city was established by J. F. Frank in 1846, and the number of wholesale produce, hardware, and dry goods stores increased until the outbreak of the Civil War. The wholesale firm of B. Lowenstein and Brothers, opened in 1861, was one of a number of firms that would influence Memphis for generations.

As in all Southern cities of the era, there were slave traders. The firm of Bolton, Dickens, and Co. was the early leader in the Memphis slave market. Its leading role was captured, however, by Nathan Bedford Forrest, later to be a feared Confederate cavalry leader in the Civil War. Motivated primarily by good business sense, Forrest kept his slave pens clean and dealt honestly with his customers. By the late 1850s he was selling about a thousand slaves annually, enough to make him one of the largest and richest slave traders in the South.

The fact that ante-bellum Memphis was considered to be as much a town of the West as of the South is not usually remembered, but, in pre-Civil War days, the frontier lay across the river in Arkansas, and Memphis occupied a strategic location in relation to Texas and the far West. It was a natural departure point for those areas, part of the reason why so many Tennesseans such as David Crockett and Sam Houston passed through as they left the Volunteer State to become part of Texas history.

In addition, Memphis' location on the Mississippi gave it an interest in regions beyond the South. The River, and the volume of traffic that traveled upon it, tended to connect the Northern and Southern states that lay along its course. In this way, Memphis developed ties with areas of Minnesota, Iowa, Ohio, and Illinois.

Relations with the West and the upper Mississippi Valley were emphasized by the railroad and trade conventions held in the city in the late 1840s. These conventions, highlighted by the Western and Southwestern Convention in Memphis in 1845, demanded that certain improvements, such as better roads and adequate care of the river channel, be carried out by the federal government. The Convention of 1845, keynoted by John C.

THE EARLIEST PICTURES of Memphis were sketched by Charles Lesueur, a French artist living at New Harmony, Indiana, who made them during trips to the Fourth Chickasaw Bluff in 1828, 1829, and 1830. Long unknown to Americans, the sketches were discovered in the Museum at Le Havre, France, in 1969 by Prof. James Roper of Southwestern at Memphis. This is the way the Memphis downtown area looked from near the present site of City Hall on April 17, 1828. The view is northward past present Poplar Avenue, marked by two dead trees, to the row of buildings along the Market Street area. (Roper)

THE MEMPHIS WATERFRONT in June 1830 gave an indication of the continuing growth of the city. Emmanuel Young's warehouse and store (center), built in 1829 immediately after Young bought city lot No. 4, just north of where Jackson Street ended, had been improved. Constructed along both the bottom and the top of the bluff, the warehouse received freight from steamboats, which, by means of block and tackle, was raised to the upper level for storage. To the left stood a building owned by Thomas D. Carr, and the one to the right belonged to Patrick Meagher. Steps provided access between the top and the bottom of the bluff. Stacks of wood at the landing were sold to steamboats needing fuel. (Roper)

Calhoun, pressed the demand for the construction of a transcontinental railroad, thus stimulating interest in Memphis and leading to the beginning of the city's rail network.

Memphis' links with the West were demonstrated by another event, the construction of the Memphis Navy Yard. Increasing tensions with Mexico in the late 1830s had led to a greater concern for the protection of the Gulf of Mexico and the Mississippi River area from possible attack from the West. Two men, Matthew F. Maury and Maj. Gen. Edmund P. Gaines, proposed that Memphis, because of its location, play a role as an anchor of American defense in the Southwest. They accordingly pressed for the development of a naval yard in Memphis, over three hundred miles from the sea and, in 1844, the bill providing for its construction was passed.

From the beginning, the navy yard was plagued with problems. Construction proceeded slowly; Navy personnel assigned there grumbled and complained about being stationed

NASHOBA, a plantation colony located east of Memphis inside the present city limits of Germantown, was one of the most ambitious undertakings in the ante-bellum South. It was founded in 1825 by Frances Wright *(right)*, a wealthy young woman from Scotland whose ideas and actions were more than a century in advance of her time. Determined to solve the slavery problem by educating slaves and allowing them to earn their freedom, she established Nashoba (the Chickasaw word for wolf) to put her ideas into practice. Fanny Wright, a woman of remarkable attractiveness and audacity, won the friendship and aid of such men as Lafayette, James Madison, Thomas Jefferson, and Andrew Jackson. Her experiment, however, was unsuccessful. This sketch *(below)* of the plantation was probably made during the 1820s. (TSLA-Roper)

THE FIRST CHURCH BUILDING in Memphis, at 204 North Second Street, was in use in 1832 by the First United Methodist Church. The first Methodist services in the city had been held in 1826 by a circuit rider. This building was replaced by another chapel in 1845. (MPL)

so far from the sea. In 1854, Congressional dissatisfaction with the yard reached such levels that a bill was passed to give the property back to the city.

So ended the Memphis Navy Yard. In its years of existence, only one ship was produced, and that ship, the *Allegheny,* was less than successful. On its first trial run down the Mississippi, the warship's crew was annoyed by boys in skiffs who rowed around the ship, laughing at its wallowing progress. On its shake-down cruise, the *Allegheny* was forced to put into port at Norfolk, Virginia, for repairs. It was soon condemned, and never left the Norfolk harbor.

Upper-class Memphians during the 1840s and 1850s strove to create a level of society worthy of their new wealth and power, but the formation of a social structure was hampered by the rapid influx of people from the more settled states. Since Memphis, due to its recent founding, had no old-line aristocracy, wealth and honor became the basis for the new Memphis society. This emphasis led to the creation of mansions such as that built at 494 Beale by H. A. Littleton in 1858, which featured giant walnut doors that joined living room, parlor, and hall. When the doors were swung back, Memphis' largest ballroom was formed.

Ante-bellum Memphis society was dominated, however, by cotton planters from the outlying areas who would migrate to town during the winter months to live in seasonal homes or in hotels. With their balls and parties, they and their families turned the Gayoso Hotel into the winter headquarters of Memphis social life.

The unsettled nature of the city's class structure led to the great emphasis on individual honor. In an era when many younger sons of established families in the more settled

[22]

states inherited nothing but the family name, real or imagined insults to that name became grounds for conflict. Memphis therefore lived by the code of the duel until the late 1850s, and Foy's Point, across the river in Arkansas, became the gentry's dueling ground.

In the 1850s, the local newspapers began to wage a campaign against this practice. Growing ridicule of it was shown in a duel between Asa Thomas and Robert McCrary in 1857 in Raleigh Springs. When the signal to fire was given, Thomas fell and opened a bottle of red ink he had hidden in his shirt. Aghast, McCrary fled to Arkansas, where he lived for three months before discovering the trick. With charades such as this, dueling fell from grace by the time of the Civil War.

Immigrant populations were in greater number in Memphis during the 1850s than at

THIS PAINTING by J. H. B. Latrobe, probably made north of Court Square when he visited Memphis in 1832, was generally believed to be the oldest painting of the city until Dr. James Roper discovered the Lesueur sketches in France in 1969. The boat at the right is the *Steward*. Some of the virgin forest that originally covered the bluff is still evident, and only a few buildings are in sight. Memphis' total population at this time probably included less than one thousand people. (MPL)

any other time. In 1860, thirty-six per cent, or 18,000, of the white population was of foreign birth. Of that number, 4,000 were Irish and about 1,500 were German.

The Irish tended to settle in the area known as "Pinch," a district of lower-class workers. They encountered opposition from some Memphians, who were influenced by the Know-Nothing movement that swept America in the mid-1850s. In August 1854, the arrival of two hundred Irish to labor on the railroads caused Mayor A. B. Taylor to call out the militia to deal with possible trouble. An editorial in the *Appeal,* forerunner of today's *Commercial Appeal,* protested this attitude, and noted the great services of the Irish on the railroads and other laboring sites in the area.

DAVY CROCKETT, a congressman from Tennessee and a hero of American folklore, was a frequent visitor to Memphis, where he enjoyed the hospitality of the old Bell Tavern and other saloons. His first entrance into the city was dramatic: He entered the city naked, after swimming ashore when the flatboat on which he had been sleeping sank. It was from Memphis, following a political defeat, that he left Tennessee for Texas and the death and fame that would come to him at the Alamo. His parting remarks to the Volunteer State reportedly were, "Tennessee can go to hell. I am going to Texas." (TSLA)

THE FIRST BANKING HOUSE in Memphis may have been this structure located at Winchester and Main, although several early merchants performed banking services for their customers. This building was occupied by the Farmers and Merchants Bank, which was in business from 1834 until 1848. This photograph was made later. (MPL)

MEMPHIS' FIRST SCHOOLMASTER, Eugene Magevney, was a young Catholic immigrant from Ireland who began teaching elementary grades in a log cabin in Court Square during the 1830s *(above)*. At this time the square, like almost all of the Memphis area, was overgrown with large trees. Unsuccessful attempts had been made by others in about 1830 to start a school, but Magevney was the first to establish one on a continuing basis. He was also a supporter of the first public school, started in the city in 1848. (MPL)

SISTER MARY AGNES, a Dominican nun who later bequeathed about $1,000,000 to a Galveston convent, was a daughter of Eugene Magevney. Mr. Magevney's influence as a major supporter of the Catholic Church was continued by his family. (MPL)

THE OLDEST HOME in Memphis is probably Eugene Magevney's home on Adams *(below)*. Built during the 1830s, it was bought by Magevney in 1837. The first Catholic Mass in Memphis was said at his home in 1839. During the following year, the first Catholic wedding in the city took place here when Magevney was married to Mary Smith who had just arrived from Ireland. Open to the public, the house is now maintained by the Park Commission. (MPL)

THE MEMPHIS NAVY YARD was sketched by a visiting artist in 1853. Strange as it may seem for
an inland city, Memphis was the site of a navy yard during the 1840s and 1850s. Mainly the product
of ambitious city leadership and influential politicians, the Memphis Navy Yard secured regular federal
expenditures in Memphis for about a decade, but only produced one warship in its years of operation.
The ship was the *Allegheny,* launched with considerable fanfare, but disappointing in its performance.
Almost too sluggish to travel, the warship was declared unseaworthy on its maiden voyage and scrapped.
(MPL)

[26]

MEMPHIS AT THE AGE of thirty-five had grown from a hamlet of a few dozen log cabins to a bus-
tling Southern commercial city. This lithograph was made by a visitor to the city in 1854, and was
published in Dusseldorf, Germany, after his return there. The steamboat *Hiram Power* was a regular on
the River; but pictures of sailboats in use at Memphis are not common. During this decade, Memphis
experienced a business boom as the cotton lands around it were developed, and the city's population
increased from 8,841 to 22,623. When the next federal census was taken Memphis had become the
sixth largest city in the South. This picture was made when the church spires were still the tallest structures on the Memphis skyline. The southern end of Mud Island is noticeable at the left of the steamer.
(MPL)

MEMPHIS WAS A WESTERN as well as a Southern city during the ante-bellum era, as this sketch made in 1855, indicates. The view is north along the promenade—the riverside area which the original proprietors of the city stipulated to be maintained free of commercial development and available for public use. In addition to the usual cotton carts and bales, this sketch shows several covered wagons pulled by oxen and horses. Memphis was the place where many westward-bound settlers crossed the Mississippi for Arkansas, Texas, and other new locations. (MPL)

[27]

SAINT PETER'S CATHEDRAL, the oldest Catholic church in Memphis, was completed in 1854. It was built around a smaller church that had been erected in 1842. When the new building was almost finished, the older one was disassembled and removed. This example of mid-nineteenth century architecture is still in use today. (MPL)

A RIVER DISASTER occurred at Memphis during the early morning on December 3, 1855, when the steamer *George Collier,* recently arrived from New Orleans with passengers and a large cargo, caught fire and burned to the waterline. The fire also spread to the wharf boat *Mary Hunt* and the steamer *Mayflower.* In this sketch, flatboatmen are steering their vessels away from the inferno. (MPL)

THE FIRST MEMPHIAN to be elected governor of Tennessee was James C. "Lean Jimmy" Jones. Inaugurated in 1841, he was the second Whig governor of the state; but his greatest service may well have been his work as promoter of railways, including the Memphis and Charleston Railroad which was completed in 1857, two years before Jones' death. (TSLA)

ISHAM HARRIS was the second of four governors from Memphis. Tennessee, at the beginning of the Civil War, had many characteristics of a border state; and its citizens voted in February 1861 against leaving the Union. The influence of Harris, a West Tennessee plantation owner and slave holder, was important in leading the Volunteer State out of the Union and into the Confederacy in April 1861. Tennessee's devastation in the war is in part a memorial to the leadership of this governor. (Wade)

Decades of Disaster:
War, Reconstruction, and Plague

MEMPHIS RESIDENTS had good reason to be pleased with their city's progress at the beginning of the 1860s. It was the sixth largest city in the South and the largest inland cotton market in the world. Surpassing its early rivals in West Tennessee, it had become the largest city in the state.

Transportation problems had been solved with the completion of the Memphis and Charleston Railroad and the beginning of a more extensive web of railways that would connect the Bluff City with even wider markets. On the basis of trends, it seemed that Memphis could expect continued growth and prosperity as King Cotton extended his dominions throughout more of the hinterland. Memphians had no way to know, as they entered the 1860s, that they were to experience two decades of disasters. Ahead of them lay secession, war, invasion, occupation, the Reconstruction, and plague.

As throughout America, growing debate over the possible secession of slave states stirred fierce controversy. The city at first was not overwhelmingly in favor of secession. Even the election in November 1860 of Abraham Lincoln, considered by many Southerners to be the enemy of their way of life, did not immediately place Memphis in the secessionist camp. The end of December 1860 saw pro-Union and pro-secession groups holding rallies there on consecutive days, both attended by thousands. In February 1861, citizens answered a call for the state's convention regarding secession by giving the pro-Union delegates a majority of 722 votes.

Following Lincoln's inauguration, the fall of Fort Sumter, and Lincoln's call for troops, the support in Memphis for secession grew rapidly. Indeed, by this time it was a center of pro-secession fervor. Many, including almost all of the city's merchants, went so far as to advocate that the city secede from Tennessee and become part of Mississippi if Tennessee did not secede. On June 8, 1861, when Tennesseans voted to secede by 108,418 to 53,336, only five Memphians voted against withdrawal from the Union.

THE CONFEDERATE GUNBOAT FLEET on the Mississippi, commanded by J. E. Montgomery, is shown in the upper picture at Fort Pillow about June 2, 1862. By the next day the garrison started evacuating the fort and the fleet withdrew to Memphis forty miles down the river. The lower picture shows the fleet of Union ironclads, called "Pook's Turtles" for Samuel Pook who planned them, following the Rebel boats down the River toward Memphis. They are passing abandoned Fort Randolph, only a few miles above the city. These vessels soon anchored and spent the night four miles from Memphis. (MPL)

The rest reacted enthusiastically to the decision and to the subsequent outbreak of hostilities. Many military companies, such as the Emerald Guards, were formed. It is estimated that from fifty to seventy were organized in all. Memphians also responded by working in the munitions factories, taking the place of the skilled mechanics who had gone North. Several thrift campaigns were started to encourage citizens to save supplies for the Confederate armies. Early optimism concerning the short duration of the war limited their success, however.

Maj. Gen. Gideon Pillow, head of the Army of Tennessee, made Memphis his headquarters. The Confederate Congress was also concerned with the city's defense; in August 1861 it appropriated $125,000 for the building of two gunboats to protect the city from Union attack by way of the Mississippi River.

The early months of the war did nothing to diminish the belief that the Civil War would quickly end in Confederate victory. The Rebel triumph in the Battle of First Bull Run, July 21, 1861, led Memphians to name a street then at the eastern boundary of the city "Manassas," after the site of the battle.

Events in early 1862, however, brought knowledge of the possibility of Southern defeat. After the capture of Nashville, state government was moved to Memphis, operating from a building on the northeast corner of Second and Madison.

In the spring of 1862 Memphis was slowly cut off from other parts of the Confederacy, and following the Battle of Shiloh, April 6, 1862, the Memphis and Charleston Railroad was under the control of the Union Army. On April 25, Admiral David Farragut

THE BATTLE OF MEMPHIS *(above)* began at dawn on June 6, 1862. The Confederate fleet of eight converted steamboats in a double line of battle faced a line of five Union ironclads with two rams in position behind them. The battle started slowly, with the Union commander, Capt. Charles Davis, backing his vessels down the river into the fight so they could escape if necessary. After a rapid charge by the two rams, the battle became general, and by 7:00 a.m. all Confederate gunboats had been sunk or disabled except the *Van Dorn,* which escaped. The sketch below shows the end of the last surviving Confederate boat, the *Jeff Thompson,* which had drifted burning toward President's Island when her magazine exploded. (MPL)

broke through Confederate defenses, capturing New Orleans. A fleet of Union gunboats, assisted by ground forces under the command of Gen. Ulysses S. Grant, was making its way down the Mississippi toward Memphis, crushing Rebel forts that lay along the River. On June 4, 1862, Fort Pillow, about forty miles north of Memphis, was evacuated by the Confederates. The possibility of a battle for control of Memphis became an inevitability.

Two days later, June 6, the battle for Memphis occurred. The Confederate gunboat fleet, under the command of Capt. J. E. Montgomery, decided to meet the Union fleet, commanded by Col. Charles Ellet, in front of the city. Thousands of Memphians lined the bluffs, awaiting the spectacle and confident of Union defeat.

The two river forces were about evenly matched, although the Union force had more ironclads and rams—fast ships with a pointed prow for cutting into enemy vessels. After an exchange of cannon fire, the two fleets clashed in a close range battle, and the Union fleet slowly gained the upper hand. Confederate mishaps hastened their defeat. For example, the Confederate *Beauregard* steamed to ram the Union *Monarch* but missed and rammed the Rebel ship *General Price,* instead.

The mood of the crowd on the bluff quickly changed to despair as the fleet was destroyed. The explosion of the *Jeff Thompson* near President's Island, which made some Memphians think an earthquake was occurring, punctuated the defeat of the Confederate force. Only the *Van Dorn,* carrying $200,000 worth of gunpowder and supplies, escaped.

That afternoon, a small party of Union soldiers landed and proceeded to the Federal Building, then on the northeast corner of Jefferson and Third. Accompanied by the hisses of a growing crowd, the United States flag was raised over the city. Memphis had fallen.

The *Appeal,* Memphis' leading paper of the time, refused to submit. On the day of the city's capture, the staff of the paper took its equipment and fled to Grenada, Mississippi. From there, it was forced to flee to Jackson, Mississippi, then Atlanta, Georgia, and finally, to Montgomery, Alabama. The *Appeal* kept printing Confederate news until captured in the waning months of the war.

Memphis suffered relatively little under Union occupation. Only in the last year of the war was the city government replaced by martial law under the Union commander. A new factor in Memphis following its capture was the large number of Yankee merchants and speculators who followed the Union army into the city. Their willingness to trade or sell to anyone with merchandise or U.S. currency was a continual irritation to the Union commanders.

Indeed, the importance of Memphis after its capture lay in its role as a major center of illicit Confederate trade and as a continued source of supply for the Rebel forces. At the time of the city's capture by the Union fleet, the unsettled conditions associated with military turmoil had caused a temporary depression of the city's economy, but Union policy in the early days of the occupation brought it back to life. Trying to win loyalty, the Union commander allowed a free flow of goods from Northern merchants and kept

THERE WAS NO MILITARY RESISTANCE by land to the Union capture of Memphis. The dashing Confederate commander, Gen. Jeff Thompson, wearing a sash and sword, had watched the river battle from horseback on the bluff. After seeing the sinking of the River Defense Fleet, he left hurriedly "to pay a note in Holly Springs, Mississippi," and Memphis was undefended. The citizens contented themselves with curses and one pistol shot when Charles Ellet, a Union medical cadet of the ram commanded by his father, removed the Confederate flag and raised the Stars and Striped over the post office. (Harper's)

trade restrictions to a minimum. As Memphis recovered, shipments of supplies began finding their way to bands of Confederate soldiers and traders lurking outside the city.

When Ulysses S. Grant took over the command of Memphis in late June 1862, he decided that an easy way to stop this open trade with the Rebels was to expel all those with ties to the Confederacy. He accordingly ordered everyone with relatives in the Confederate army to leave within five days. Grant himself left before the order could go into effect, however, and William T. Sherman, his successor, decided the best way to stop the smuggling was to check outgoing traffic, limiting traffic to five roads and posting guards to search suspicious-looking loads. This plan was defeated by corruption because a bribe in the hands of a Union road guard was usually sufficient to allow a cargo to pass through the checkpoint.

One of Sherman's biggest problems with Memphis trade with the Confederacy was caused by cotton and the greed of Yankee speculators. When approached by an out-of-town farmer wishing to sell his cotton crop, the speculators were glad to go along with the farmer's desire to be paid in gold or silver. The farmer would then take the gold or silver to Rebel leaders, who would use it overseas to purchase guns and ammunition. When Sherman banned the use of gold or silver in transactions, farmers began trading

A CITY UNDER SIEGE was shown in this picture of Memphis during its last days as a part of the Confederacy. Union armies, after their bloody victory at Shiloh, held the area east of the city on the bluffs while Union gunboat fleets were moving down the Mississippi River from the north. Snags and

their cotton to Yankee speculators in Memphis in return for salt, desperately needed by the Confederate army.

In a further attempt to slow down the pace of the smuggling, Sherman ordered the first of a number of bans on goods that could be shipped from the city. The transfer of guns and ammunition was forbidden completely, drugs and medicines could be sold only in limited quantity, and salt and salt meat were required to be registered before they could leave the city.

As Union trade regulations in Memphis grew stricter, more ingenious methods of smuggling were used. Joseph H. Parks reports several: When one lady attempting to pass the lines was asked to alight from the carriage, the difficulty with which she complied aroused suspicion; a search revealed that beneath a huge girdle she had tied twelve pairs of boots each containing whiskey, military lace, and other supplies. A Negro woman was caught with a five-gallon demijohn of brandy underneath a loose-fitting calico dress and suspended from a girdle at the waist. Dead animals, their bodies filled with packages of quinine and other contraband goods, were dragged by smugglers to the boneyards outside the city. On at least one occasion, the hearse of a funeral procession bore a coffin filled with medicine for Gen. Earl Van Dorn's army.

The River continually posed an easy avenue for contraband. Planters would travel to Memphis, place orders for excessively large numbers of supplies, and ship the supplies on the Mississippi to their plantation. From there, the goods would be dispensed to Confederate forces. These practices were curtailed somewhat by later Union orders limiting the amount of goods that could be purchased.

Some steamboats would leave Memphis loaded with goods and cruise up and down the Mississippi so that Rebels in small boats could come alongside to transfer a portion of the cargo. These steamboats would also rendezvous close to streams, meeting there with smaller craft that would carry the cargo up the tributaries to waiting Confederate forces.

Smuggling out of Memphis was often conducted on a large scale. Rufus Joiner, drowned while passing goods across to Arkansas, had an order worth over $100,000 found on

small boats are visible in the River; and behind it stands the city, with the Navy Yard on the left and the Gayoso House with its white columns at the right. This sketch was published in *Harper's Weekly* on May 31, 1862. One week later the city had fallen. (Harper's)

his body. The owners of Ward and McClellan, a prosperous Memphis pharmaceutical company, were imprisoned and their stock was confiscated. After taking their oath of allegiance to the Union, they were estimated to have smuggled over $60,000 worth of drugs and other medical supplies to the Confederate armies.

Only the most stringent Union methods, which brought the whole economy of Memphis to a halt, had any great effect on the smuggling, until, finally, in the last months of the war, as the hopelessness of the Confederate position became clear, there was a drastic drop.

As the Confederacy slowly collapsed in 1863 and 1864, loyal Memphians received little word to lift their spirits. Often, the exploits of Nathan Bedford Forrest, a Memphian and a famous Rebel cavalry leader, provided the only favorable news. Despite his lack of formal military education (or perhaps because of it), he became one of the nation's most effective military leaders. and the only one ever to rise from private to lieutenant general in a single war. So effective were his campaigns that they have been studied by military leaders of many nations, including the German General Staff before the blitzkrieg of Europe in World War II. One of Forrest's enemies, Gen. William T. Sherman, described him as "the most remarkable man our Civil War produced on either side." Forrest's reputation in Memphis reached a peak in August 1864 when he led a brilliant raid on Union forces in the city itself.

Leaving a number of troops at his base in Oxford, Mississippi, as a screen, Forrest secretly led about 2,000 troops toward Memphis and, around three o'clock on Sunday morning, August 21, reached the outskirts of the city, which had been under Union control for over two years, and did not expect attack. Despite his orders for stealth, Rebel yells soon rang out as the Confederates advanced into the city that was home for many of them.

Forrest's brother, Capt. Bill Forrest, led a group of scouts to Gayoso House, where Gen. Stephen A. Hurlburt was quartered. In his urgency to capture the Union general, the Confederate captain rode his horse into the lobby, demanding the whereabouts of the

[35]

general from a startled night clerk. Fortunately for General Hurlburt, he was away from his quarters that night and thus avoided capture.

Jesse Forrest, another brother, commanded a group sent to capture Gen. Cadwallader Washburn. The yells and shots of the Confederates alerted Union sentries, who awoke the general in time for him to escape by running through the streets in his night clothes.

The elder Forrest and his men withdrew by 9 a.m., cheered by ladies of Memphis who leaned out windows to salute the passing Rebel troops. Union pursuit was beaten back, and Forrest retired with six hundred Federal prisoners. He later returned General Washburn's uniform, which had been taken in the raid on his quarters.

Memphis at the end of the Civil War provided the setting for one of the greatest naval disasters of recent history when the river ports of the South were crowded by Union troops anxious to return home. As the steamboat *Sultana* stopped at Vicksburg, going upstream, over 2,000 Union ex-prisoners of war came on board, making a load of over 2,500 people on a boat with a legal capacity of 396. The load proved to be too great for the ship's engines and, on April 27, 1865, the *Sultana's* boilers exploded. The ship sank about seven miles north of Memphis.

Memphians learned of the disaster when the following dawn allowed them to see bodies and pieces of wreckage floating down the river. The total of 1,450 casualties made this the worst peacetime naval disaster until the sinking of the *Titanic,* in which 1,513 were lost.

Since Memphis had been captured without siege, it avoided the destruction that had befallen many Southern cities. Its strategic location had helped keep trade alive, though on a diminished scale, during the war years. So Memphis did not have to completely begin anew after the Civil War. The city suffered, however, from the destruction that had occurred in much of the surrounding area where battles and skirmishes had destroyed many farms and trampled much of the farm land. The major source of Memphis' cotton trade and the destination of the city's distribution market, therefore, was greatly reduced in the post-war period.

The end of the war brought marked changes to Memphis' population, with many blacks, freed from slavery during the war, coming to the city in search of work. In the decade from 1860 to 1870, their number increased from 3,882 to 15,741. Increased racial tensions, caused by the new relationship between the recently freed blacks and whites anxious to continue their pre-Civil War dominance, were aggravated by the absence of jobs for blacks. Unable to find work, the newcomers soon encountered difficulties in merely finding food and shelter, and crime increased as many of them struggled to survive. The rise in crime affected Memphis whites, intensifying their already present distrust and fears.

These tensions between blacks and whites caused a year of small incidents between April 1865 and April 1866. On May Day 1866, another small incident occurred when two buggies, one driven by a black and one by a white, collided, with the two drivers beginning to insult each other and soon fighting. The brawl was watched and cheered by a large

SOLDIERS OF OCCUPATION took charge of Memphis following Mayor John Park's surrender after the Battle of Memphis in 1862. Their commander was tough but honest Gen. William T. Sherman *(right),* who took forceful action against smuggling and corruption by Northern and Southern profiteers alike, and who tried to restore as much civil power as possible to the mayor. These soldiers in Court Square *(above)* were examining the bust of Andrew Jackson that secessionists had defaced by removing Jackson's words, "our Federal Union: It must be preserved." (Harpers-MPL)

group of black soldiers who had recently been discharged as troublemakers from the Union garrison in Memphis, where their white accusers had been less than impartial. As the fight was being broken up by police officers, the black soldiers began to protest. Rocks were thrown toward the policemen and shots were fired. Who shot first is not known.

This entanglement touched off a three-day race riot, in which the predominately Irish police gave active support to their fellow whites, who were led by Irish from the "Pinch" and other outlying areas, as well as by a few city officials. When the rioting stopped,

NATHAN BEDFORD FORREST, Memphis' greatest military leader, was also one of the most successful businessmen in the city during the ante-bellum era. Born in Middle Tennessee in 1821, he had to assume the heavy responsibility of helping his mother care for eight younger brothers and sisters after his father died when Nathan was sixteen. After experience as a farmer and livestock trader, he moved to Memphis in 1851, where he continued his activity as a stock trader and established a slave-trading business. By the beginning of the Civil War, he had served as a Memphis alderman and had become the wealthiest slave trader in the Southwest. (MPL)

[38] FORREST'S CAVALRY attacked Irving Prison in order to force the withdrawal of a large Union army that had advanced from occupied Memphis into Mississippi. Forrest led 2,000 picked troops around the federal force to assault its headquarters in the city. Arriving in Memphis at 3:15 in the morning on August 21, 1864, Forrest's command completely surprised the enemy. Although the Confederates were not able to free the prisoners at Irving, they captured 600 Union prisoners and took them back to Mississippi. (Harper's)

forty-four blacks and two whites were dead, hundreds of people had been wounded, and over one hundred black-owned buildings, including twelve schools, had been destroyed. The resulting federal investigation gave Memphis a bad reputation throughout America, and caused many Northern Republicans to call down on it a yet harsher Reconstruction, the political process which was meant to aid the seceded states in rejoining the Union, but which actually took on an unpleasant social, as well as political nature.

Alone among ex-Confederate states, Tennessee's reconstruction was handled by a government of Tennesseans, elected by residents of the state. Memphis suffered, however, because the government was controlled by Radical Republicans from East Tennessee, where a great majority had remained loyal to the Union during the Civil War and resented the planters and politicians of the rest of the state, whom they felt had dragged the state into war. William G. Brownlow, Radical Republican leader and governor of the state during the late 1860s, tried to make Reconstruction in West and Middle Tennessee a harsh experience for the ex-Confederates.

Reconstruction franchise acts reduced voting rolls and increased Brownlow's support by disenfranchising almost all who had actively supported the Confederacy. The granting of the franchise to blacks in 1867 also strengthened the Radical Republicans, infuriating the ex-Confederates. After the granting of the franchise, Memphis blacks were at first content to vote for Brownlow's candidates and for Northerners who moved to the city after the war. Led by a black named Ed Shaw, however, many of them began to press for the election of black candidates and, from 1869 until the Southern whites regained political control of the city around 1875, they met with some success. In 1872, two blacks were elected to the City Council. In 1874, the peak Reconstruction year for black electoral success in Memphis, Ed Shaw was elected wharfmaster and six blacks were elected to the City Council.

Governor Brownlow and the Tennessee Republicans also used other means to increase their control. In May 1866 the Metropolitan Police Act was passed, partly as a result of the race riot earlier that month. This act gave Governor Brownlow control over appointments to and actions of the police departments in Memphis, Nashville, and Chattanooga.

The governor and his party furthermore reorganized the courts of Memphis, bringing them under closer political influence. When Matt Galloway, editor of the *Avalanche,* a rabidly anti-Republican Memphis newspaper, attacked Judge William Hunter, a carpetbag Republican from Illinois, a notable confrontation occurred. After the editor attacked Judge Hunter's abilities and heritage in vivid, passionate language, Judge Hunter responded by citing Galloway for contempt, and finally had him jailed. At first, Mr. Galloway succeeded in smuggling some editorials out of his jail cell, but after this was prevented, editorials written by his wife and by his co-editor continued the assault against the judge.

Many ex-Confederates, disenfranchised and chafing from their lack of political power, turned in these years to the newly formed Ku Klux Klan, and Nathan Bedford Forrest, once again a resident of Memphis, was its first leader. Judge Hunter was consequently

THE MEMPHIS RACE RIOT of 1866 was the most violent civil conflict that has occurred in the city. Started by a traffic collision of two hacks on May Day 1866, it developed into three days of lawlessness and disorder by rampaging mobs. Members of the police force joined in the riot, and order was restored only after the city was occupied by Union troops. Freedmen's schools, which had been educating the newly freed blacks, were particular targets of the rioters. (Harper's)

AT LEAST FORTY-EIGHT PERSONS, mainly black, were murdered, and hundreds were wounded. Robberies, rapes, and arsons took place without interference. Large numbers of former slaves had gathered in the city after the close of the Civil War. Against a background of burning buildings, this Northern artist's sketch, which is probably accurate, shows blacks being shot down in their homes and in the streets. (Harper's)

A NEW COURT appeared in Memphis after the Freedman's Bureau was established by Congress in March 1865 to supervise the transition from slavery to freedom by the blacks in the South. The Bureau provided limited relief and education services for the freedmen, and also undertook to regulate their labor contracts with white employers. In this scene, an unhappy employer has apparently been brought before the Bureau by the former slaves standing behind him. The plaintiff is fortunate to be accused at this time, for this drawing appeared in *Harper's Weekly* on June 2, 1866; and the Bureau was not given an authority by military commission to try persons accused of depriving freedmen of civil rights until July 16, 1866. (Harper's)

threatened by reputed Klansmen during his conflict with editor Galloway. The amount of Klan activities in Memphis is believed to have been limited, however, most of it taking place outside, in the rural areas of West and Middle Tennessee.

As the 1870s began, Memphians confidently looked toward a decade of rapid growth for their city. William G. Brownlow's influence in their government had been broken, and the mid-South was rebuilding from the ravages of Civil War. Despite this early optimism, the 1870s were to be disastrous, ending with the surrender of the city's charter in 1879.

Problems of health would play a major role in the sudden decline of the city. Sanitary conditions in Memphis during the 1870s were atrocious. The water supply was drawn primarily from shallow wells, and the mixing of water from the wells and from sunken cesspools that dotted the city was common. The corporate area was drained by the Gayoso Bayou, which by the 1870s had become a "series of stagnant pools, separated by dams of decaying organic matter and human excretement," according to Dr. Gerald Capers in his *Biography of a River Town*. No wonder Memphis had been attacked in earlier decades by plagues of cholera, dengue, dysentery, and smallpox.

Yellow fever, or "yellow jack," as it was then commonly known, was the disease that was to cripple Memphis in the 1870s. The city was located in a low, swampy area, an excellent breeding ground for the *Aedes aegypti* mosquito, the deadly carrier of yellow fever, and the still waters of the Gayoso Bayou plus the town's open cesspools provided additional breeding grounds.

The fact that no one at this time knew the cause of yellow fever increased the potential of disaster. Scientists held varied opinions, while some doctors felt that the disease came from breathing a tiny organism into the lungs and thus into the blood. Other doctors argued that it was caused by the noxious fumes rising from the city's streets.

Memphis had had small outbreaks of yellow fever before the 1870s, but in 1873 the first major epidemic hit the city. In early August, two men sick with the fever were put ashore in Happy Hollow, a poor Irish section of town, from a steamer bound north from New Orleans. The spread of the disease then followed a familiar and almost-inevitable pattern: The two men had been bitten in the tropics by mosquitoes infected with the yellow fever virus, and now all mosquitoes that bit these men would become its carriers. The sickness was immediately transmitted thus, and quickly spread through the Irish section of Memphis.

The rarely active Memphis Board of Health announced on August 14 that yellow fever was epidemic in the city, and by September, 25,000 of the 40,000 inhabitants had fled. As for the rest, at the peak of the epidemic in early October, fifty or sixty were dying daily, until a series of frosts in late October killed the mosquitoes, ending the epidemic. Five thousand of the fifteen thousand people who had remained in the city had become ill, and two thousand of them had died.

By the new year, businessmen had returned to Memphis and the city again took on an air of normality. But an underlying feeling of fear and tension existed during the next few years. Citizens realized that, at any time, a new epidemic could force them to leave the city. As a result of this, though annual trade rose, Memphis real estate values dropped, and the population of the city did not increase.

The dreaded yellow fever returned in 1878, its return marked by the death of Mrs. Bionda, wife of an Italian store owner, on August 13. Although the overly cautious Board of Health did not declare an epidemic until August 23, Mrs. Bionda's death started a frenzied exodus from the city that even included most of Memphis' Protestant ministers. People packed trains, overloaded boats, and crowded the roads in their panic. The citizens of many towns such as Jackson, Tennessee, fearing the plague would spread to their communities, refused to allow the fleeing Memphians to enter. Despite such precautions, cases of the fever were carried as far away as Chattanooga.

One month after Mrs. Bionda's death, only 19,000 of Memphis' 40,000 citizens remained in the city. Of this number, 14,000 were blacks, who felt they were immune to the virus. To their chagrin the blacks found that, for the first time since yellow fever had come to Memphis, they too were susceptible.

Many individuals worked heroically during the epidemic to care for the sick and comfort the dying. Members of the Howard Association, a group of Memphians organized during an 1867 epidemic to care for the sick, labored mightily. The Catholic clergy

ROBERT R. CHURCH, Sr. *(right)*, one of the most successful business-men in the history of Memphis, also was reported to be the first black millionaire in the South. Born in 1839 at Holly Springs, Mississippi, he worked on several steamboats until the Battle of Memphis on June 6, 1862. During the battle he escaped from the steamer *Victoria*, on which he was serving as steward, when it was captured by the Union fleet. Taking advantage of his experience on the River, he went into business in Memphis. His commercial activities were invariably successful. He op-erated a restaurant, a saloon, and a hotel which he built on the corner of South Second and Gayoso streets. These successes led to others. Since there were no public recreational facilities for black citizens, he established them himself, creating Church's Park and Auditorium on Beale Street in 1899 *(above)*. Seven years later, he opened the Solvent Savings Bank and Trust Company, described as the first bank for blacks to be initiated in Memphis *(below)*. When the city was reorganized after the disastrous yellow fever epidemics, Church bought the first $1,000 bond issued by the city. He continued to be a Memphis business leader until his death in 1912. (RRC)

performed many heroic acts of kindness. During the height of the epidemic, people died in such numbers that their bodies outstripped the supply of coffins and they were buried in shallow trenches, often lying where they had died for several days as a result of the backlog caused by the heavy casualty rate.

When the first frosts of October ended the epidemic, 5,150 people were dead. But the damage to the city in 1878 included more than the number of deaths. Its business climate had suffered once more, since citizens were afraid to start new projects. Many of those who fled this time did not return to the city, much of the German population moving to St. Louis. The fever had struck particularly hard among the Irish, of whom many had been too poor to leave during the epidemics. Their reduced numbers greatly diminished the role of the Catholic Church, and as Memphis became increasingly provincial during the 1880s, the cosmopolitan voice of the church was missed.

Memphis had entered the Reconstruction era with a large city debt. All during the 1870s, its citizens struggled with plans to reduce it or evade it, but financial crisis was to be the second great catastrophe to hit them. There were several reasons for the large indebtedness, the amount of which reached almost four million dollars in the early 1870s:

In 1867, the city government had decided to improve the streets, which were then composed of layers of mud of different consistency. It signed a contract with a Mr. T. E. Brown to pave the streets with Nicholson pavement, a series of wooden blocks. In a couple of years, the pavement began to rot and decay. When the city tried to stop payment, Mr. Brown took the city to court. In a series of decisions reaching to the U. S. Supreme Court, Memphis was forced to pay Mr. Brown and other contractors. This number of large payments, plus the cost of repaving the streets and payments for certain other rebuilding that had to be done after the Civil War, contributed to the size of Memphis' debt.

The city's officials at this time were extremely corrupt. Lodged in office in a tight ring that even several reform mayors were unable to break, they demanded large kickbacks on almost all public contracts and business, and so their inefficiency and criminality added to the city's debt. In addition, the nature of Memphis's population aided the increase of indebtedness. Many citizens were too poor to pay any taxes at all; yet certain basic services were provided them without charge.

As the decade began, Memphis was unable to pay the interest on its indebtedness. Federal judges were granting judgments against the city that allowed its creditors to collect money from its merchants before the city government could take the money in as revenue. Memphis mayors made several trips to New York, trying to persuade the creditors to accept less than their full interest payments.

By 1874 the business community realized that the city's future was at stake. The Memphis Cotton Exchange, the Chamber of Commerce, and the Peoples' Protective Association (formed in 1874 specifically to fight for repeal of the city's charter) began to explore ways to deal with the indebtedness. Slowly, a consensus began to form that

JOHN GASTON, a young French immigrant who served in the Confederate army, settled in Memphis in 1865. After he had worked as a bill collector and a chef, friends helped him open his own restaurant in 1867. During the yellow fever epidemic he used his profits to buy land at low prices; the income from his real estate and other enterprises made him one of the richest men in the city. Throughout his life he maintained his reputation as one of the finest chefs in Memphis. His generosity was responsible in part for the establishment of Gaston Community Center on South Third Street. John Gaston Hospital is also named for him. (MPL)

NAPOLEON HILL, a youth of poor background and limited education, left Memphis in 1850 to join the Western gold rush. In 1857, at the age of twenty-seven, he returned to Memphis with $10,000 he had made in California. With this capital he entered business as a cotton factor and, when he married soon afterward, his wife's parents gave him a $25,000 wedding gift. He was absent from Memphis during the Civil War because he was a supporter of the Union, but he returned to build a remarkably successful business empire. He soon owned the third largest cotton-factor and supply business in the world, handling millions of dollars worth of cotton annually. During this time, Memphis was the largest inland cotton trading center in the nation. (MPL)

THIS IMPOSING PALACE, built by Napoleon Hill, "The Merchant Prince," was public evidence of his success. After becoming a millionaire in the cotton business, he helped form the Union Planters Bank, which has been successful as a Memphis institution to the present. With profits from these enterprises, Hill expanded his investments into insurance, real estate, other banks, mines, and railroads. His home was at the corner of Third and Madison where the Sterick Building now stands. (MPL)

VICTORIAN VILLAGE, a historic district on Adams Avenue from Neely to Orleans streets, was the location of some of the finest residences built in the city after the Civil War. The Mallory-Neely House *(above)* was built in 1860 of painted stucco over brick. The Fontaine House *(below)* was built ten years later. Both are now open to the public during regular hours. The Village, featuring various styles of architecture from about 1840 to 1890, is a favorite site in Memphis for walking tours. (MPL)

repeal of the city's charter, which would place the area under the direct control of the state, was the best solution. Impetus was given by the yellow fever epidemic of 1878, which further demoralized the citizens of Memphis. On January 31, 1879, Governor of Tennessee Albert S. Marks signed the bill to dissolve the charter of Memphis and place the city under the direct control of the state, with the name "Taxing District of Shelby County."

THE PEABODY HOTEL has been a major landmark throughout the history of Memphis. The old Peabody was located on Main Street at the northwest corner of Monroe in 1878. (MPL)

MEMPHIS' FIRST PUMPING STATION, built in 1873, supplied muddy water from the Wolf River for use in homes and businesses. This system, although unsanitary, was probably no worse than Memphis' previous source, which consisted of shallow wells dug by individual users in a municipal area filled with cesspools and garbage dumps. This station was built by a private enterprise, the Memphis Water Company, in which the city also was a stockholder. It was located on the south bank of Wolf River near its mouth. (MPL)

MARDI GRAS was celebrated in Memphis during the decade from 1872 to 1882. Organized like many other activities in the city for the promotion of business, it was started by a campaign in the old Memphis *Appeal*. The first "Fat Tuesday" celebration featured three thousand horsemen (some dressed in medieval costumes) and was attended by a reported twenty thousand people. Unfortunately, during this decade the city was nearly destroyed by fever epidemics, and Mardi Gras was abandoned in 1882. (MPL)

NEW COTTON FIELDS were cleared in the Memphis trade area as plantations expanded into the swamps and forests. The deep alluvial soil of the Mississippi Valley was some of the best in the world for growing cotton. In their rush to plant larger crops, planters sometimes deadened the trees by gird-ling the bark with axes and planted cotton rows around the standing trunks. This well-hoed field *(above)* had been planted on new ground. Each autumn armies of pickers *(below)* moved through the fields pulling the cotton and stuffing it into sacks slung over their shoulders. (MPL)

[49]

HOPEFIELD, on the right bank of the Mississippi across from Memphis was poorly located, as most of its area was subjected to regular flooding by the high water. It has since been replaced by the town of West Memphis, which is several miles away from the river bank. The Fourth Chickasaw Bluff, on which Memphis is located, is far above the high water level, but the Arkansas side of the River has always been low. Since there was no bridge over the Mississippi until more than twenty years later, passengers for Little Rock and Hot Springs crossed the River by ferry to take the train to Hopefield. (MPL)

WHEN YELLOW FEVER struck in 1878, more than half the population of Memphis (about 25,000 of them) fled in panic in all directions. Many of them, already infected, carried fever germs in their blood to be spread by other mosquitos wherever they went. Pariahs, the refugees from the yellow fever were feared and rejected by all. Free movement in the area became impossible, since Memphis for a time excluded travelers, and other cities and towns refused to accept people from Memphis. Many who had fled were driven into the swamps where they camped in isolated area. Eventually, about 5,000 found safety in camps organized for them. (MPL)

NUNS AND PRIESTS performed sacrificial service when the disaster struck the city. Following the first death on August 13, most of the Protestant ministers and some of the doctors fled the city. Many of those who stayed were the poor Irish, who were mainly Catholic, and the blacks. Of those who cared for the sick and dying, many themselves caught the fever and perished. (MPL)

MORE THAN 5,000 people died of the less than 20,000 who remained in the city. Grave digging was almost the only activity that prospered, as people died faster than they could be buried. The County Undertaker kept four furniture wagons in constant service, but even these could not collect all the bodies. About twelve thousand who had suffered from the disease recovered. (MPL)

Rebirth of a River Town

UNDER THE TAXING DISTRICT arrangement, the state of Tennessee collected all taxes, and drew up a budget allocating expenditures for the area. The act provided that management would come from two boards of commissioners, four of whose members would be elected and three appointed by the governor. This was the forerunner of the commission form of government that would run Memphis until 1966.

Although the city did not completely escape its debt by means of the Taxing District, it did succeed in removing the immediate pressure for payment. The municipal debt was later refunded at a lower rate. The budget allocation from the Taxing District did allow improvements in sanitary conditions, and community services that greatly reduced the threat of disease and improved the national reputation of Memphis. In 1880, the city began installing a sewer system, eliminating the need for open cesspools and the dumping of wastes in the Gayoso Bayou (later covered and made an actual sewer drain). In 1887, an ice company discovered artesian water below the city, bringing about a solution to the city's pure water problem. Memphis still draws its water from artesian wells.

Under strong leadership, primarily from businessmen, the city's Board of Health began to take a more active role in disease prevention. Plumbing inspections, limited vaccinations, and garbage service were all instituted in the 1880s. Despite pressure from some in business, a scientific quarantine system was also introduced to keep diseases from reaching the city.

By the time Memphis' charter was restored in 1893, its economic recovery was well under way. The building of railroad lines, which had stalled with the onset of the Civil War, began again in the 1880s. In that decade seven new lines reached the city. In 1892, a railroad bridge across the Mississippi was completed, the only one south of St. Louis. The rapid growth of the city's population (from 33,000 in 1880 to 102,000 in 1900) was reflected in the growth of the outlying areas, and the growth in population of the entire mid-South increased the importance of Memphis as a distribution center. For example, in 1891 the city was the fifth largest wholesale-grocery market in the United States.

Cotton continued to be the number-one product through the rest of the century, even though the Civil War and Reconstruction had brought changes to the business. The latter part of the nineteenth century saw the rise of the tenant farmer and of the cotton factor, exemplified in Memphis by Napoleon Hill. Supplying the planter with almost all his needs, from seed to equipment to food for the workers, the cotton factor received his profit from the interest he charged the planter.

Lumber became an important business in Memphis during the late 1880s. As the great forests of the East and upper central regions of the nation became used up, lumbermen turned toward the Southern forests. The lumber market in Memphis was slow to grow, however, because the money of Memphians was tied up in cotton. Eastern money, therefore, was used to build and operate the sawmills that dotted the banks of the Wolf River toward the close of the century.

As the nineteenth century drew to a close, marked changes in the city's population were evident. Blacks constituted a greater percentage than ever before, by 1900 comprising 50,000 of the city's 102,000 citizens. With the exception of a few businessmen such as Robert R. Church, Sr., they were at the bottom of Memphis society. Memphis whites attempted to ignore them and their problems by social and economic repression, but the reckoning could only be delayed. The problems remained for the twentieth century.

The composition of the white population had also changed, with the city no longer having sizeable ethnic minorities. The Irish and German communities that existed before the yellow fever epidemics were not replaced. Instead, the 1880s and 1890s saw a great immigration from North Mississippi and West Tennessee. It seemed as if a whole generation from surrounding small towns and farms had moved to Memphis in search of better jobs and the excitement of city life. In 1898, fifty-two percent of white parents in Memphis had been born in other parts of Tennessee or in Mississippi, and only two percent had been born in the city. So, in many ways, it was a new Memphis that greeted the twentieth century. Much of the brawling and diversity that had characterized the city's youth were gone.

A COTTON PLANTERS' CONVENTION, promoted with considerable fanfare, brought together the men of the old South to deal with a new problem. The bearded gentlemen met at Memphis in 1881 to consider the serious financial plight of cotton. Despite all the publicity, they achieved nothing, for their industry continued to practice uncontrolled and excessive production in an economy that was increasingly controlled by large economic powers outside the agrarian South. E. C. Morehead was a leader of the movement. (Harper's)

COTTON WAREHOUSES were an important link in Memphis' dealings in the staple fiber. Sometimes it was necessary to hold the cotton bales at the city until transportation to outside markets was available; occasionally the cotton would be held until prices improved; in all cases, the fees for cotton storage and handling were a major source of income for the city. Bales were moved within the warehouses by mules and black laborers. This picture was made about 1895. The clothing suggests cool weather, but the empty space in the warehouse indicates that it is late in the season—perhaps late winter or early spring. (MPL)

OFFICERS of the Lee Steamboat Line, standing on a platform of cotton bales, watch while rousta-bouts load their boats on the Memphis waterfront. The steamer visible in the foreground is the *Sadie Lee,* with the *Harry Lee* in the background. It is apparently a winter day with the wind blowing across the river from the west. This Memphis company became the largest steamboat line on the Mississippi. (Wade)

THE STEAMBOAT *T. P. Leathers* entered Memphis Harbor with one of the largest shipments of cotton ever seen at the city. The lower decks were almost under water from the weight of a reported 4,000 bales of cotton. Such an excessive, but profitable, load was hazardous to carry—particularly in rough water. A previous record had been set by the steamer *Chickasaw* in 1885. (Wade)

THE FAMOUS LUXURY PASSENGER STEAMER *Robert E. Lee* is moored to the Memphis wharf in a strong north wind. Logs and debris floating by in the background indicate that the river was in flood stage and rising. The *Robert E. Lee* received national attention during her race with the *Natchez* up the Mississippi River in 1870. (Wade)

THE U. S. SNAG BOAT *Macomb,* steaming down the Mississippi, represented a major activity of the federal government to aid river transportation, impeded when the powerful action of the current some-times caused large sections of river bank to cave in. The trees that fell at the same time would float along, lodging finally in shallow waters. Most of their limbs would break off eventually, and these and the trunks, often hidden under water, provided snags that sank many boats. The snag boats either pulled up and removed the snags or cut them off deep under water. (Wade)

PURE ARTESIAN WATER, located in a vast deposit of water-bearing sand about five hundred feet beneath the city, was an unknown resource until 1887. Against the advice of many "experts," the first well to this depth was contracted for by Richard C. Graves, the owner of an ice plant near Gayoso Bayou. After the first clear water geysered from his well, there was no possibility that residents would continue to be content with water from Wolf River. The following year, rival water companies organized into the Artesian Water Company, which built new pumping stations and began laying additional pipe. From this time the city has had a healthful supply of water. The coal-powered pumping station, shown in 1899, was part of the system which the city purchased four years later. (MPL)

THIS HORSE-DRAWN PUMPING WAGON, photographed in front of Station No. 4 of the Memphis Fire Department, was the latest fire-fighting equipment in 1899. (MPL)

MASS TRANSIT was by mule car in the 1880s *(right),* but electric trolleys *(below)* were put into use in the 1890s. In both types of streetcars, the passengers were protected from the elements, but the operators were partially exposed to the weather. The mule driver, Colbert Woods Shoults, later served as a deputy Sheriff of Shelby County. (MATA)

THE GAYOSO HOUSE (shown in 1899) was probably the Memphis hotel best known both to local residents and travelers during the nineteenth century. An elegant white-columned structure facing the River, it was surrounded by trees on three sides when it was opened by Robertson Topp in 1846; but the city quickly grew up around it. (Harper's)

THE OLD EXCHANGE BUILDING was constructed when businessmen organized the Memphis Cotton Exchange in 1884. Realizing the importance of successful agriculture to business profits in the city, the Cotton Exchange supported both diversified farming and improved methods of cotton production. One of the more impressive buildings in the city at the turn of the century, it was replaced by the present Exchange Building in 1910. (C of C)

THE APPEAL BUILDING at the corner of Main and Jefferson was the home of the *Commercial Appeal* until 1906, when the newspaper moved to Second and East Court, where it remained until it went to its present site (the old Ford plant) on Union, about 1934. (MPL)

HORSES AND BUGGIES were still in evidence on the cobblestones of downtown streets in 1895. This view is eastward on Madison Avenue from the U. S. Post Office. (MPL)

BUSINESS CONTINUED as usual on Main Street at Court Square in 1883, with trolley cars, horseback riders, delivery wagons, and cotton carts and wagons in evidence. But, here, the large and expectant crowd, with some looking from windows, suggests a holiday is being observed. The sign at the northwest corner of Main and Court announces "Football Today," and the six-mule coach carrying musicians seems to be a part of the celebration. The building on the right is where the Lincoln American Tower stands today. (MPL)

JEWISH SYNAGOGUE.

CHRISTIAN CHURCH.

CALVARY EPIS. CHURCH

FIRST BAPTIST CHURCH.

SECOND PRESB. CHURCH.

FIRST METHODIST CHURCH.

MEMPHIS CHURCHES were impressive architectural landmarks in the downtown area by the last decade of the nineteenth century. This illustration shows six selected churches as they appeared in 1895. (MPL)

MRS. HIGBEE'S SCHOOL FOR GIRLS stood at the southeast corner of Beale and Lauderdale. In 1888, when this picture was made, this section of Beale Street was occupied by respectable businesses and expensive homes, despite the notoriety that was associated with the portion of the street nearer the steamboat landing. (MPL)

MEDICAL EDUCATION, of varying quality, has been available in Memphis throughout most of the city's history. In 1894, the curriculum was much shorter and less complex than it is today, as is indicated in this announcement of the Memphis Medical College. The cause of yellow fever would remain unknown until early in the next century. (MPL)

FIFTEENTH
ANNUAL ANNOUNCEMENT AND CATALOGUE
OF THE
MEMPHIS HOSPITAL
*
MEDICAL COLLEGE

THE NEW COLLEGE BUILDING.

SESSION 1894-95.

LECTURES BEGIN MONDAY, OCTOBER 1, 1894, AND CLOSE LAST OF MARCH, 1895.

SAINT MARY'S SCHOOL FOR GIRLS in 1895 was located on Popular Avenue at Orleans, adjoining Saint Mary's Cathedral. It has since moved to Perkins Extended at Walnut Grove. (MPL)

THIS CHRISTMAS DISPLAY of fresh meat was arranged at Sites & Ames' Fulton Meat Market in 1893. Blocks of ice stood on the corner, and the butchers and other employes of the market are lined up for a picture. This is the Second Street view of the business. The arrangement seems to include beef, mutton, and fowl. Although considered unsanitary today, this method of display allowed customers to inspect their purchases before buying. (MPL)

[64]

EFFORTS TO INCREASE the speed with which horse-drawn fire engines could respond to calls reached a peak during the 1890s. All of the Fire Department's horses could not be kept constantly hitched to the engines, and so the firemen suspended the harnesses for Engine No. 6 from the ceiling, which meant that a team could be moved into place and its gear lowered and buckled on in minimum time. (MPL)

ELMWOOD CEMETERY, opened on July 15, 1853, is the city's oldest cemetery still in active use. These pictures, made in 1895 *(above)* and 1900 *(below),* show a use of ornate and impressive monuments which still is characteristic of the location. Burried here are two Tennessee governors, James C. Jones and Isham Harris, and one of the proprietors of Memphis, John C. McLemore, who bought Andrew Jackson's share of the original John Rice grant. Fourteen Confederate generals and many other veterans of the Civil War are buried here also. The cemetery occupies about eighty acres and has had more than seventy thousand burials. (MPL)

[65]

[66]

SUBURBAN PASSENGERS to Raleigh could ride Memphis Street Railway Car No. 3 in 1895. At this time, there were still extensive wooded areas between the two locations. Raleigh Springs Inn, a grand hotel and favorite spa of the mid-South, stood on a hill on the north side of the Wolf River. The water of the springs, which have dried up because of a general lowering of the water table in the area, was considered salubrious. And the lush, carefully tended surroundings allowed guests to take a relaxing stroll in a grove of oak and cedar trees. (MPL)

THIS STEAM DUMMY ENGINE is shown in use at a wood yard near East End Park about 1888. The young man standing in the center is James Maddux who, after this start in railroading, later spent sixty-two years working for the Illinois Central. As the city grew in population during the late 1900s, the supplying of coal and wood for fuel supported large businesses. (MPL)

"CASEY" JONES at the throttle is shown in this artist's picture of the famous engineer. It was on April 29, 1900, that John Luther "Casey" Jones left the Illinois Central Depot at the corner of Poplar Avenue and Front Street driving Engine 382, pulling the "Cannonball" to the fatal wreck that made him a part of American song and folklore. (CA)

THE COMPLETION of the first bridge across the Mississippi River at Memphis on May 12, 1892, created a long-deferred link in the national transportation system. Standing by Engine No. 9 of the K.C.M. Railroad are four participants. The men on the left and right are unidentified, but the two in the center are (left to right) Harry Litty and John J. Quinn. Litty served once as mayor of Memphis. (MPL)

EAST END PARK, one of the commercial amusement areas in the city, originated as part of a fifty-acre tract bought in 1889 by the East End Railway. The pavilion, seen in this photo made in 1895, was used for vaudeville performances and other attractions. The site, on the north side of Madison between Morrison and Diana, is partially occupied by a dairy today. (MPL)

THE PAVILION at Jackson Mound Park provided a place where a generation of city residents spent happy evenings before the city park system was established. This view was eastward up the river bank in 1895. Opened on July 4, 1887, this commercial recreation park was named for Andrew Jackson, one of the original proprietors of the city. The pavilion opened with a May Day celebration each year and remained open until the fall weather became too cool. Band concerts provided alternate two-steps and waltzes for the guests, and special celebrations were held each Fourth of July and Labor Day. The downtown ten-acre tract was bought by the Memphis Park Commission in 1912 and renamed De Soto Park the following year. Although the site provides an expansive view of the Mississippi River, it receives comparatively little use today, since most residential areas have moved away. (MPL)

ELEGANCE in the 1890s often assumed the form of heavily ornamented interiors of public buildings and conveyances. These guests are sitting in one of the grand rooms of the Mississippi River steamboat *Great Republic*. Some of the steamers were as luxuriously carpeted and furnished as the best hotels. (MPL)

UNION AVENUE, here fringed by trees and grapevines on a fall day in 1895, extended westward toward the business district. The narrow, unpaved lane was used by pedestrians and horse traffic. Today, this area is buried under a wide expanse of asphalt. (MPL)

THE MEMPHIS BLUFFS, their banks not yet reinforced by concrete, were relatively undeveloped at the beginning of the twentieth century. Framed by the Frisco bridge, they were photographed from the Arkansas side, almost a mile away. Then, as now, farm land was in use just across the River from the city. (C of C)

THE DOWNTOWN BUSINESS DISTRICT in the 1890s included a crowded commercial area on the east side of Front Street and a newer section along the railroad lines at the bottom of the bluff. This early afternoon view is north from the Government Building at the west end of Court. (MPL)

Memphis Becomes a City

MEMPHIS ENTERED the twentieth century larger in population and area than ever before. The census of 1900 listed its population as 102,320, although this figure was later said to be inflated by about 20,000. The physical limits had been extended in 1898, increasing the size of the city from four to twelve square miles. Some land was annexed in 1898 which included large wooded tracts, as well as many residential areas.

To provide for an orderly pattern of development, the city's first Board of Park Commissioners was formed in 1900, and one of its first acts was to oversee the purchase of a 335-acre tract then located in the city's extreme northeast corner. This tract was given the name of Overton Park, in honor of one of the founders of Memphis. Riverside Park was also soon purchased and developed. In 1902, the Park Commission oversaw the start of an ambitious parkway system, designed to circle the city on three sides with scenic routes. North, South, and East parkways, which followed the contemporary city limits, are the result of this plan.

The 1900s saw the beginning of the transportation revolution. Automobiles, the first one believed to have come to Memphis in 1901, were no longer an unusual sight on Memphis streets by the end of the decade. Streets were beginning to be planned with their use in mind. Airplanes also began to appear. The National Aviation Meeting held in Memphis in 1910 did much to stir the interest of city residents in the new mode of travel.

In 1903, residents began one of their periodic attempts to "clean up" the city. Gambling houses were closed, as had happened before. The city's gamblers were not worried, since the houses were usually allowed to quietly reopen after a few weeks. This time, however, the houses stayed closed for almost a year, which led the desperate gamblers to plead to the city council, promising to run sedate establishments and citing the money they brought into the city. A further blow against suspected vice was struck when the Tennessee General Assembly outlawed horse racing in 1905, causing the rapid decline of the racing park in nearby Raleigh Springs.

Following the formation of the privately owned Memphis Artesian Water Company, citizens had complained they were being charged excessively high rates for water service.

Since Memphis had been given the right in 1898 to control its own waterworks, debate over municipal ownership of the water supply had grown with the new century. A committee formed in 1902 recommended that the city purchase the waterworks and so, in early 1903, plans to do so were put under way.

The same decade saw a rapid increase in other community services. When the newly annexed areas of the city, made up of more square miles than the entire old Memphis, demanded that city services be brought to them, sewer pipes were laid there and also in uncompleted sections of the old city. Street paving and repaving continued, this time with granolith blocks being used, and the Memphis police and fire departments received new equipment, including call boxes placed strategically around the city, to improve police communication. Toward the end of the decade, the fire department began purchasing motorized fire engines. The day of the horse-drawn fire steamer was drawing to a close.

In 1909, commission government formally came to Memphis, with a board of five commissioners to be elected, and one of the five to be mayor. The first mayor under this system was a mild, seemingly unimpressive man named E. H. Crump. Defeating a challenge in the courts to the validity of his election, he would remain in office until 1914, and boss of Shelby County politics until his death in 1954.

A WELL-DRESSED COUPLE in the early twentieth century watches the Mississippi River from Bluff Park. The park was located south of Union Avenue where it turned down the bluff toward the River. Cossitt Library and the post office are in the background. (MPL)

THE OLD ILLINOIS CENTRAL RAILROAD cotton platform and team track about 1905, looking north: Behind the men checking the cotton bales is the St. L. IM & S Freight Depot. It was later acquired by the Missouri Pacific Railroad. The building at the left was the old L. N. & O. T. Freight Depot, later a part of the Illinois Central line. It was later used by the Cudahy Packing Company until it was destroyed in a fire. (MPL)

THESE COTTON BALES are stacked outside a warehouse on the north side of Calhoun Street west of Main. The streetcar track was the old Jackson Mound line which turned left, toward the north, on Main. Out of sight at the right of the photograph was the old Illinois Central depot. In 1900, streets that were paved were sometimes covered with the mud carried over from other, not yet improved, streets. (MPL)

AN ARCH OF COTTON BALES was erected at Second and Madison for visitors to the Confederate Reunion in 1909. Decorations in Memphis have often featured its most valuable product. The business in the right background belongs to the Vaccaros, one of the city's earliest successful Italian immigrant families. (MPL)

THE LAST HORSE-DRAWN fire steamer bought by the city of Memphis was driven down Main Street by veteran driver Richard Barner. This sturdy model represented the acme of horse-drawn pumping machines. Motor vehicles were already in use when it was purchased in 1910. (MPL)

GARBAGE COLLECTION, performed in the early days of the city by herds of pigs, became a municipal function as a result of increased concern for public health after the great yellow fever epidemics. This garbage collection wagon was in use near the turn of the century. (Evans)

THE TENNESSEE CLUB BUILDING was one of the imposing structures of the downtown area at the turn of the century. The building, at the northwest corner of Second and Court, is now owned by the law firm of Burch, Porter, and Johnson. (MPL)

LUXURIOUS INTERIORS were found in Memphis around 1900 in the buildings owned by social clubs. This room was located in the Chickasaw Guards Club and Grand Opera House. The volunteer companies by this time no longer had a military function, but they continued as social organizations. (MPL)

THE ELKS CLUB CARNIVAL was getting under way at Main and Jefferson around 1905, as members of the band assembled in front of the Equitable Building. Today, the admission charge of ten cents to the carnival and street fair would be considered a bargain. After the Equitable Building burned in 1906, Bry's store moved to the site from its former location at Main and Adams. The Lowenstein Building stands now on the original site of the Equitable Building. (MPL)

THE DR. D. T. PORTER BUILDING, an eleven-story brick structure, was one of Memphis' early skyscrapers. In 1900, trolley cars carried the mail to the suburbs. Billiard parlors, or pool halls, were common recreation centers frequented by men only. This view is northeast from the corner of Main and Madison. (MPL)

THE MEMPHIS SKYLINE in 1907 was beginning to rise above the level of the three- and four-story buildings that had made up most of the business district in the late nineteenth century. Using steel-frame construction and electric elevators, builders found it possible to erect towers to new heights. The Porter Building in the center foreground was the first of these, but by this time it was flanked by the Tennessee Trust Company Building on the right and the Bank of Commerce Building on the left. (MPL)

CONFEDERATE PARK at the beginning of the twentieth century provided a view up the Mississippi River. These trees, fully grown today, had recently been planted when this photo was made. (TSLA)

A STREET SCENE in the downtown business district in 1900 included heavy traffic by cotton carts. The electric street lights hanging over the intersections were to be replaced within a few years by newer globes on posts placed at the corners of sidewalks. (CL)

COURT SQUARE, although one of the city's smaller parks (2.07 acres), may well have been enjoyed by more people than any other in the Memphis park system. Laid out when the city was surveyed in 1819, it has been in the downtown business area to the present. Located on Court Street, between Main and Second, it is still a favorite site to stroll, eat lunch, or feed the squirrels and pigeons. These gentlemen, photographed in 1900, were probably businessmen who had offices in the vicinity. (MPL)

THE ORIGINAL "Mr. Crump" song, which later became the "Memphis Blues," was played first by this band at Main and Madison in 1909. W. C. Handy, who was brought from Clarksdale, Mississippi, to organize the band, is noted by the arrow. The drummer at the right is Alex Dukes, father of Laura Dukes. (HEG)

MAIN STREET in 1902 was still dominated by streetcars and buggies. Although the first automobile had been brought to Memphis a year earlier by Samuel Carnes, horseless carriages were still curiosities on the streets. This view is north across the Madison Avenue intersection. (CL)

MALCOLM R. PATTERSON, the third Memphian to serve as governor of Tennessee, held office from 1907 until 1911. One of the few powerful governors of the state during the twentieth century, he was a leading opponent of Prohibition before its passage in 1909, but later became a lecturer for the Anti-Saloon League. Two of his children and a granddaughter still live in Memphis. (TSLA)

MAYOR OF MEMPHIS at the age of thirty-six, Edward Hull Crump was on the way to becoming the strongest political leader of Tennessee during the twentieth century. Born in Marshall County, Mississippi, in 1874, he came to Memphis in 1893 with a ninth-grade education, but with an unusual degree of ambition and determination. (MPL)

ARMED LEVEE GUARDS were organized to prevent cutting of new levees. As the system was being built early in the twentieth century, it protected some lands while diverting larger amounts of flood waters onto others. Since owners whose lands were subject to flooding sometimes opened the levees to relieve the pressure of water, those who owned property on the safe side of levees organized for protection. Many of these men are armed with shotguns, the most common weapon in the area. (BW)

DREDGING OPERATIONS to keep the Mississippi River channels open became more necessary as traffic on the waterway increased. The federal government, which had earlier assumed responsibility for clearing the River of snags, was engaged regularly in removing sand and mud from the channels by the early twentieth century. The crews lived on the boats for long periods of time, as is indicated by laundry (including long underwear) drying on the upper deck on a wintry day. (MPL)

THE MEMPHIS WATERFRONT was often crowded with steamboats by the early 1900s, when this picture was made. Steamboat traffic had been increasing for several decades as the population and commerce of the valley grew. These roustabouts are unloading freight from the *J. N. Harbin*. The *Sadie Lee* is in the background. (MPL)

MEMPHIS BEGAN, in the new century, to recover from its disasters of the 1880s. This early morning photo shows only light traffic on Main Street in front of the Menkens Building. (CL)

AN AIR SHOW held in Memphis in April 1910—only seven years after the Wright brothers flew the first plane!—aroused great curiosity, and crowds gathered in large numbers. It often presented a problem to get the crowds to make room enough to let the fragile planes take off. (MM)

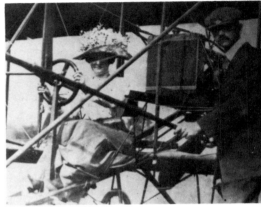

GLENN CURTISS, later a nationally famous leader in aviation, was responsible for bringing the National Aviation Meeting to Memphis for four days of flying. He is shown here with his wife. The plane seems to be fitted with an automobile steering wheel. (MM)

CRASHES WERE COMMON at the air show, although there were no fatalities. In one accident, a Curtiss biplane piloted by C. C. Mars crashed on a car in which Mrs. Ernest Ritter of Marked Tree, Arkansas, was sitting while watching the show *(left)*. Both were injured. Takeoffs always involved suspense. The photo below shows Glenn Curtiss beginning to rise from the ground. (MM)

The City Completes a Century

DURING THE FOLLOWING ten years, the unpredictable nature of the Mississippi River gave Memphians some problems. Floods, especially the ones of 1912 and 1913, inundated many sections of the riverfront area, particularly in low-lying North Memphis. Public pressure for an adequate levee system grew, but no definitive action was taken.

Improvements were made in the city, however. The first public swimming pool was opened in 1912, and the city's first municipal golf course was built in Overton Park. With the increasing presence of the automobile affecting the city, the Harahan Bridge was opened in 1916, to provide for both railroad and automobile traffic. The Frisco Bridge, built in 1892, before the era of the automobile, had not been designed with automobiles in mind.

As was the case throughout the South in this era, blacks were not expected to take part in the political process (except as blocs of votes to be manipulated by white leaders). Robert R. Church, Jr., a successful black businessman and leader in Memphis, determined to correct the political lassitude of his race by personally forming, and largely financing, the Lincoln League in 1916. Before it ended in the 1920s, the Lincoln League had become a nationwide organization which had successfully encouraged blacks to register and to vote, drawing attention to the problems of blacks and proving itself as a force in national Republican politics. In 1917, Robert R. Church, Jr., also organized the Memphis chapter of the National Association for the Advancement of Colored People (NAACP).

World War I increased the always-present patriotic fervor of Memphians. War-bond drives were held, and politicians thrived on appeals to patriotism. Germantown changed its name to Nashoba for the duration of the war, and Park Field in Millington was used by the U. S. armed forces as a training camp for pilots. Although not used during the 1920s and 1930s, Park Field would reopen in World War II as the Millington Naval Air Base.

As Memphis celebrated its Centennial in 1919, its citizens could look back on a remarkable hundred years, although the potential exhibited by the river city in the 1840s and 1850s had received great setbacks during the troubles of the 1860s and 1870s. The recovery begun in the 1880s, however, continued through the Centennial, with lumber and cotton the basis for a revived economy.

Growth in both size and population had occurred at a rapid pace after the plague years, especially in the early twentieth century. Marked improvements in city sanitation and services had effectively removed the threat of another epidemic like the one that had nearly ruined the city in the 1870s. Memphians in 1919 could take pride in their city's rebound from disaster.

CROWDS OF PEDESTRIANS and numerous trolley cars crowded Main Street in 1912. Automobiles, although beginning to appear in the city, were still scarce enough that none are visible in this picture. By this date, streetlights had been moved to the corners of intersections where they were placed in clusters. Some of the businesses visible in this view—such as Pantaze, Brodnax, and the Robinson Drug Company—are still operating in the city. (MPL)

ONE OF THE EARLIEST NIGHT VIEWS of downtown Memphis was made in 1911. The view is south on Second Street from Court Square, which is in the right foreground. Court Street extends eastward between the building containing Hill's Business College and the Commercial Appeal Building. (MPL)

SNOWFALL AT CHRISTMAS in Memphis is not common, since the coldest weather is usually in January and February, and most snows occur during these months. This snow scene was photographed in the woods of Overton Park on Christmas Eve 1914. (MPL)

OVERTON PARK ZOO was started without planning or preparation in 1905 when a black bear which was a mascot of a Memphis baseball team was chained to a tree in the park because there was no other place to keep him. The Memphis Zoo Association was organized soon afterward, and other animals were acquired during the next few years. The Carnivora Building *(above)* was opened before 1910. Adequate space for the bears was provided later. The photo of the Alligator Lake *(below)* was made about 1914. (MPL)

THE THOMAS W. MARTIN Meat Market, about 1911: The owner's son, T. S. Martin, later owned a meat market on South Main. Most of the meat on display is pork, which was the meat most often used in the city. (CR)

EARLY LONG-DISTANCE TELEPHONE SERVICE was provided to Memphis callers by this pay station of the Central Telephone and Telegraph Company in the pre-World War I era. Miss Willi McCandless, the operator (sitting at the right), collected fees from and placed calls for the waiting customers. When she had their parties on the line, they took the calls in one of the numbered booths in the background. Miss McCandless, who had also worked for the Chisca and Peabody hotels, died in 1959 at the age of eighty-two. (PDC)

MISSISSIPPI RIVER FLOODS brought a special irony to residents of Memphis. At these times, the River which had made the bluff a suitable site for a city brought destruction to it. The flood of 1912 caused extensive damage. A freight train *(left)* at the rear of Gayoso Oil Company was caught by rising waters; a streetcar *(below)* moved through water over Main Street by the city gas works. As the April floods continued, scaffolds *(bottom)* were erected to provide walkways for pedestrians. (MM)

AS THE WATERS of the 1912 flood continued to cover low-lying areas of the city, the residents resorted to various aids to their travel. Boats, like the one in the foreground fitted with a shortened chair, were used to travel along the streets. Substitutes for sidewalks, such as the plank walkways in the background, connected the houses to one another. People in these areas had to move out of their houses or into second-floor rooms. This picture was made near Market Street landing on April 6; the dress and the uniform age of the passengers suggests that they are schoolboys. (MPL)

BRIDGES AND ROADS closed to automobile traffic by high water *(right)* could sometimes be traversed by horses and wagons *(above)*. (MM)

FLOODS IN THE GREAT VALLEY of the Mississippi continued to be a source of repeated devastation from the time that people first moved into the area until the River was brought under relative control by the building of the levee system and the completion of a series of dams by the TVA and other agencies. These refugees were photographed while waiting for a rescue boat during the flood of 1913. Mainly blacks, these men and woman gathered at the end of a levee with their baggage were probably sharecroppers and farm workers. (MPL)

REFUGEES FROM THE FLOOD of 1913 were aided by the steamer *Chas. H. Organ,* Bedding and personal possessions were piled on the dock on the foreground while roustabouts unload bales of hay. The steamboats, with their shallow draft, woulc travel through flooded areas where water was only a few feet deep. (MPL)

THE MOUTH OF WOLF RIVER became an area of substantial industrial development as the urban area to the south grew, resulting from its convenient access to the Mississippi and the relative availability of inexpensive land. This photo was made when the water was high during the 1913 flood. (MPL)

SCHOOL BUSES were in use in the Memphis area at an early date. This wagonette carried students to and from Messick School about 1913. Neither the horses nor the well-dressed students seemed to be concerned with the muddy school yard. The canvas curtains on the sides could be rolled down during rain. (MPL)

THE ADMINISTRATION BUILDING, and at that time the only structure, of West Tennessee State Normal School was under construction in 1912. Except for some additions to the back side, it remained relatively unchanged until it was renovated in 1975. Today it houses the administrative offices of Memphis State University. Surrounded in 1912 by farmland and a few residents, the school grew with the city. The university now has more than twenty-two thousand students, and the city limits have expanded several miles east of the campus. (TSLA)

THE FIRST MOTORIZED FUNERAL in Memphis was that of Chester Anderson. The procession was photographed at the entrance to Elmwood Cemetery. (Cubbins)

MEMPHIS RECEIVED occasional visits from small naval vessels because of its location on the River. The USS *Petrel* came for a visit in 1912. The ship, built late in the nineteenth century and powered by a coal-burning engine, had seen service in the Spanish-American War. As insurance, her designers had also outfitted her with sails. This official U. S. Navy photo was not made on the River, but at sea. (MPL)

THE RALEIGH BATHING BEACH on the Wolf River, located on property owned by the Lindbergh family, was a favorite recreation spot in 1915 where many people learned to swim. The rope in the tree at the left was used by swimmers to swing out and dive into the deep water below. This sandbar is west (or downtown) from the Jackson Avenue bridge. (BC)

TAPS HOLE, located north of Wolf River, was an example of some of the wilderness areas in the countryside near Memphis. Unsuited for any commercial use, it was a large area deeply washed by erosion. Austin-Peay Highway was later cut through Taps Hole. (BC)

THE LINCOLN LEAGUE, a political organization of black Republicans, was founded by Robert R. Church, Jr., in 1916 to provide united power in support of the needs of Memphis blacks. By providing voting schools and voter-registration drives, it attracted national attention and became the model which was copied by black leaders in many other cities. This rally, at Church's Auditorium, was held in 1916 when Charles Evans Hughes was the Republican candidate for the Presidency. Ben. W. Hooper, former governor of Tennessee, was the party's candidate for the U. S. Senate. (RRC)

[94]

THE HARAHAN BRIDGE, completed in 1916, was designed both for trains and cars. This view is westward along the side built to carry car and truck traffic into Memphis from Arkansas. When the Frisco Bridge (seen at left) was built in 1892, automobiles had not been invented. (C of C)

THE FEDERAL BARGE LINE terminal handled cargo for both steamers and barges at its location below the present site of the Holiday Inn Rivermont. This photograph was made on February 1, 1916, when the terminal was being inspected by a party from St. Paul, Minnesota. (TSLA)

THE COLD WINTER OF 1917-1918 was a memorable and bitter experience for people living within several hundred miles of Memphis. Although the average temperature in Memphis during winter is 42.3 degrees and the season is usually mild, there have been occasional exceptions. During December 1917, the temperature in Tennessee reached its lowest recorded level at 32.7 degrees below zero, and the temperature at Memphis remained below zero for a long period. Except for small areas of moving water, the Mississippi River froze over, as it has done about twice each century since the valley has been settled. Death among livestock and wildlife was extensive, and people and their property suffered also. In this photograph, two steamboats, the *De Soto* and the *Georgia Lee,* are being crushed in an ice gorge. (MPL)

PARK FIELD at Millington opened in 1917 to serve as a training center for pilots until after the armistice in November 1918. The 907-acre tract became a U. S. Navy airfield in 1942 after the beginning of World War II. This view is of a cadet barracks in the foreground and a mess hall at the left. (CJH)

ACCIDENTS were not uncommon among the student pilots of World War I. Airplanes such as this Curtiss JN4-D "Jenny" were primitive by present standards. The "Jenny" was powered by the famous OX-5 engine, rated at ninety horsepower, and was covered with fabric. The resulting light weight made it possible to crash into the tops of trees without falling to the ground. Careful flying was encouraged by the fact that the pilots were not allowed to use parachutes. (CJH)

COLLISION between new and old forms of transportation occurred in an airplane crash on May 19, 1918, when Lt. Joe Dawson, a pilot training at Park Field in Millington, lost control of his Curtiss JN4-D while doing aerobatics for a Red Cross rally. Falling about 1500 feet, the plane crashed on two automobiles and a horse-and-wagon. Several spectators and the pilot were injured; but the only victim was the horse. (CJH)

MEMPHIS' CENTENNIAL in 1919 was celebrated by the usual city observance, a parade. (MPL)

MEMBERS of the first Motor Truck Company of the Memphis Fire Department in 1919 stand proudly by the city's most modern fire-fighting machine, an American La France 2-2 Pumper. Automobiles, which became common in the city during World War I, had demonstrated their effectiveness; also, the increasing mileage of the city's streets had made coverage by horse-drawn machines difficult. Partial name identification from left to right indicates that the firemen are Wilhite, W. Licer, P. Miles, Capt. J. O'Neal, Loach, and Frank Milazzo. (MPL)

HORSES AND WAGONS had disappeared, and the number of automobiles had increased so much that traffic lights had to be installed on Main Street after World War I. This view is looking south, with the Porter Building on the left and the Kress store on the right. (MATA)

The Prosperous Twenties

MEMPHIS PARTICIPATED in the general prosperity the nation enjoyed during the post-World War I era, largely as a result of the increased governmental spending that had been necessary for the war effort. Growth was relatively steady, despite a minor post-war slump when the government's participation in the economy was reduced. By the time the census of 1920 was taken, the municipal population had risen to 162,351, increasing with each farm boy or girl that came into the city from rural areas of the mid-South.

Two new hotels, the Adler and the Tennessee, were built downtown. An old hotel, the Peabody, reopened in 1925 at a new location on Union Avenue, where it would remain in operation for fifty years. The Columbian Life Insurance Company was moved to Memphis from Atlanta, and other businesses opened or expanded their volume of sales and services to take advantage of the Bluff City's growing markets.

Sears Roebuck completed its new building on North Watkins in 1927. The tower of this structure became one of the most prominent landmarks of the midtown area, and Sears Roebuck at Memphis, through its catalog sales, became buying headquarters for a rural region that included several Southern and Midwestern states. Memphis thus became a trade center from which many farm and small-town families could buy without leaving their homes.

The steady eastward spread of the city continued. Areas that had once been far from Memphis found the municipality's outskirts growing around them, beginning the suburbs and bedroom communities known so well to the city planners and sociologists of today.

Another natural disaster rekindled interest in 1926 in the improvement of the river-bluff north of the city's two bridges. A large cave-in there carried hundreds of square feet of business property to the bank below and into the water. Cave-ins had, of course, occurred throughout the history of Memphis, but the concern over this particular one led to plans to end this threat to riverfront property and to stabilize the bank south of the old city waterfront. Riverside Drive was therefore started, both to relieve the growing pressure of traffic in the downtown area and to provide support for the river banks.

The 1920s also saw aviation gain a firm foothold. During 1921, Vernon and Phoebe Omlie brought their flying service to Memphis, which developed interest and enthusiasm in the new mode of travel. This, plus the realization that air traffic would soon be a national transportation feature, led to the construction of a municipal airport that was dedicated in 1929.

THIS UNUSUAL VIEW of the riverfront south of Beale Street was probably taken in the 1920s from near the present location of Ashburn Park. The Exchange Building can be seen on the skyline (center), but Riverside Drive had not been built. The water level is unusually low. (MPL)

ADAMS STREET in 1922 was paved, supplied with fire hydrants, and equipped with electric lines for the streetcars. The view is past the fire station. police station, and courthouse. (TSLA)

THE LOWENSTEIN'S BUILDING was the home of one of Memphis' most prominent department stores by the 1920s. It had grown from the wholesale firm of B. Lowenstein and Brothers, which opened in 1861. The expansion of the firm into shopping centers outside the downtown area had not yet started when this picture was made. (C of C)

THE DETECTIVE DIVISION of the Memphis Police Department was photographed in front of the Police Building on March 15, 1922. Their uniform appearance suggests that even in civilian clothes they were probably not hard to identify as policemen. They were commanded by Inspector William T. Griffin. (Thompson)

THE VICTORY PARADE still received enthusiastic support from Memphis citizens in 1922. It was organized by the Memphis Unit of the National Victory Memorial Association, and its floats were made with the help of Memphis lumbermen. The uniformed marchers were Boy Scouts. (TSLA)

BUILT TO LAST 1,000 years, Clarence Saunders' mansion involved a monumental construction project in 1922-1923. Planned while his Piggly Wiggly grocery-store empire was still growing, it was built on a 155-acre tract north of the Memphis Country Club, and cost almost one million dollars. After burning the old buildings on the site, a small army of workmen rushed the construction of the new mansion of pink Georgia marble. It was to be the finest money could buy and was to be operated by twenty-five servants. Saunders lost the property in his business failure in 1923, and since 1930 it has been maintained as a museum by the city. He named it Cla-Le-Clare, but the press and the public have always called it the Pink Palace. (MPL)

POSTWAR PROSPERITY during the 1920s led to the opening of several new hotels. The Adler Hotel *(below)* was opened in 1924, and the Hotel Tennessee *(right)* in 1927. The Adler was operated by Herman S. Adler, an immigrant from Germany who had previously owned the Adler Apartments, to the left of the hotel in the photo. The hotel was located on the south side of Linden between Main and Front streets. Adler lived at the hotel until his death in 1965. It was then purchased by John J. Hooker Enterprises, and is now owned by Hohenberg Brothers. The hotel was the residence of many entertainers, including Jack Benny and Eddie Cantor, when they were in the city. The Hotel Tennessee, located at the southeast corner of Third and Union, was also owned by Adler. It is still in operation, although under different management. During the 1920s the new Peabody Hotel was opened on the east side of Union between Second and Third streets, remaining in operation from 1925 to 1975. (BP)

AVIATION WAS BROUGHT to Memphis in 1921 by Vernon C. and Phoebe Fairgrave Omlie, two local residents who have contributed the most to it. Lt. Vernon Omlie, shown here piloting a U. S. Army DH-4, was a flying instructor during World War I, and later an aircraft salesman for Curtiss Northwest Airplane Company. Omlie's life changed abruptly in May 1921, when he met Phoebe Fairgrave, a girl who had graduated from high school a month earlier. (McWhorter)

PHOEBE FAIRGRAVE, one of the most daring women of her time, was eighteen when she graduated from Mechanic Arts High School at St. Paul in April 1921. After Working as a stenographer for a few days, she went sightseeing at a nearby airport where she quickly decided to become a pilot. While learning to fly she met Vernon Omlie, and on May 21 persuaded him to give up his job at Curtiss to fly for her. On July 10 they took off from the St. Paul airport, determined to fly the plane as high as possible. Finally at 15,000 feet Phoebe parachuted out. When she reached the ground, she held the women's world record for parachute jumping. Soon afterward, Phoebe married Omlie and they moved to Memphis, engaging in a general flying service that included aerial photography and stunt flying. Phoebe is shown here *(left)* by her plane, advertising Layne and Bolton Company, a business still active in the city. The advertisement below pictures Vernon piloting a plane, with Phoebe, who performed under her maiden name, hanging by her teeth beneath it. She did not wear a parachute. (McWhorter)

EXHIBITION FLYING   AERIAL PHOTOGRAPHY   COMMERCIAL WORK

PHOEBE FAIRGRAVE, AVIATRIX

SEE Her Hang By Her Teeth from Speeding Airplane.

Her Do a Daring Parachute Leap.

Lt. Omlie in Loops, Spins, Barrel Rolls With His Battle Plane.

CAR-AIRPLANE RACES were a public attraction in the early 1920s when both were new and relatively matched in speed. This photograph, made by Phoebe, shows the plane, which probably belonged to her and Vernon, in the lead. (McWhorter)

THIS MONOCOUPE, one of the fastest planes of its day, was bought by Phoebe and used when she entered the 1931 National Sweepstakes Handicap Air Derby which started in Santa Monica, California, and ended more than two weeks later in Cleveland. Phoebe's entry in the race was surprising to many, but even more surprising was the fact that, being a woman, she won. She was given a new Cord convertible automobile as a prize.

She later flew for Franklin Roosevelt and went to Washington with the Bureau of Air Commerce. Vernon was killed in an airplane crash in 1936, but Phoebe lived much longer, one of the few early stunt pilots who did. She was buried at Memphis in 1975. (McWhorter)

MANAGING THE AIRPORT at Memphis gradually required more of Vernon's time, while Phoebe did more of the flying. They are shown here about 1923 with an unidentified flyer (at right). Their De Haviland D-4, which was probably war surplus, is parked in high grass, a not unusual occurrence at airfields of the time. (McWhorter)

BEALE STREET during the early 1920s had many substantial businesses. This sale was being held at the A. Schwab Dry Goods Store, still in operation at 163 Beale Street by the same family that established it in 1876. (CL)

ONE OF MEMPHIS' GREATEST HEROES was a modest black laborer, Tom Lee, who on May 8, 1925, saved the lives of thirty-two people. When the U.S.S. *Norman* sank about twenty miles below Memphis, Tom took his small boat, the *Zev*, to the scene of the disaster and succeeded in carrying all the surviving victims of the steamer to shore. Tom Lee Park on the riverfront is named for him. (CA)

JUDGE CAMILLE KELLEY, a socially prominent Memphis matron, was "somewhere near the age of thirty-six" when she was appointed to the Juvenile Court by Mayor Rowlett Paine in 1920. She exercised a stern maternalism to a generation of juveniles who appeared in her court. This photo was made at Pall Mall with Bud Hall (left) and Sgt. Alvin York, the Tennessee infantryman who was probably the greatest American hero of World War I. (MPL)

THE MEMPHIS CAVE-IN of 1926 was a natural sisaster that revealed the necessity of stabilizing the bluff's banks. On July 24, a large section, weakened by water, collapsed. At the bottom of the area, near Butler Avenue *(above)*, is a conveyor shed and oil house. The gas pump and telephone pole have remained erect as the land fell away. When the property of the West Kentucky Coal Company slid away toward the River, it left a railroad track and its ties exposed. These men *(above)* are standing on what was left. That the slide might continue to adjacent areas was a more serious problem than the business losses, and this led to renewed efforts to strenghten the banks of the banks of the River with fill and concrete and to the building of Riverside Drive along the riverfront. (BW)

MEMPHIS TECHNICAL HIGH SCHOOL, constructed at a cost of $600,000, was one of the model institutions of its kind in America. It is seen here as it was when opened during the fall of 1929. The site had been occupied by the ante-bellum mansion of P. P. Van Vleet, a pioneer merchant and whole-sale druggist of the city. His widow sold the estate to the city in 1927. (C of C)

THE SEARS ROEBUCK BUILDING, completed in 1927, was the largest structure in the midtown area. It also made Memphis the center for the large mail-order business, one that encompassed a multi-state area of farms and small towns where the Sears Roebuck catalog offered the only competition to local stores with their limited selections of high-priced merchandise. (TSLA)

"SUN" SMITH, who achieved fame as a trumpeter for W. C. Handy, was born in Greenville, Mississippi, in 1894, and came to Memphis in 1915. He later played in a jug band, the Beale Street Originals, which followed the Beale Street Sheiks of Frank Stokes. When the Peabody Hotel opened during the 1920s, a large recording business was conducted there to supply new markets for black music. The extensive migration of blacks to northern cities, such as Chicago, had created a market for music which the new arrivals in the North were accustomed to enjoying. Recording companies found it easier to come to Memphis to do recording than to bring Southern musicians to the North. Smith, who became famous during this era, is still living. (HEG)

"MEMPHIS MINNIE" LAWLER, a nationally known blues singer and guitarist, was born in Algiers, Louisiana, and came to Memphis about 1900 at the age of six. One of the most popular performers during the 1920s when "race records" were being recorded, she is still an idol in Europe several years after her death. (HEG)

THE ICE MAN was a regular caller at Memphis homes before the general use of privately owned refrigerators. These deliverymen and other employes pose before the Railways Ice Company. In 1929, when this picture was made, the change from horse-drawn ice wagons to trucks had been almost completed.

[110]

THE PACKAGE TERMINAL of the Federal Barge Line was built on the River below the present location of Riverside Drive. Its loading chute led down from the top of the bluff. Freight was carried along the chute to and from the railroads at the top. (MPL)

The Thirties

AS WAS THE CASE throughout America, the great depression following the stock market crash of 1929 slowed the growth of Memphis, and the prosperity of the twenties came to an end. A sudden drop of prices brought stagnation to the cotton industry. Since the city's economy was based so strongly on the state of the cotton market, all businesses suffered. Unemployment increased, and purchasing power of the citizens declined.

Partly as a means to bring publicity to cotton and to stimulate the industry, the Cotton Carnival was begun in 1931, and proved itself early to be a success. Large numbers of people, both residents and visitors from nearby, crowded into town to enjoy the holidays. Based on the earlier Memphis Mardi Gras, the carnival featured parades, decorated river barges pulled by blacks, and cotton "royalty."

The lifestyle of Memphians did not completely stop with the Depression. The increasing use of the automobile led to a new phenomenon in the city, the drive-in restaurant, and businesses which supplied and serviced automobiles continued to grow. Federal spending, especially after the beginning of the New Deal programs in 1933, helped restore confidence and bring a beginning of limited recovery.

During this decade Memphis achieved national attention through the efforts of the city censor, Lloyd T. Binford, who banned many movies that otherwise would have been shown in the Bluff City.

As a stride in improving the welfare of the residents, John Gaston Hospital was opened in 1936, named in honor of the French chef and philanthropist who had contributed the land for the facility. The presence of the Medical School of the University of Tennessee also helped to make the city a medical center for the mid-South area.

The formation of the Tennessee Valley Authority (TVA) in 1933 started a major new federal agency that contributed to the economic welfare of a large part of the South, and also brought the advantages of cheaper electric power. In a special election in 1936,

[111]

Memphians voted to purchase the city's electrical system from its private owners and to join the TVA power system.

The last damaging flood of the Mississippi River came to the city in 1937, covering much of North Memphis with standing water. After this one, a system of levees to protect the area brought a sigh of relief.

By the end of the decade there was another relieved sigh as the problems of the Depression were being overcome and the national economy gradually improved.

THE BOY SCOUT MOVEMENT was established strongly in Memphis, supported by many residents who were interested in boys and their outdoor activities. Several scout leaders from the period beginning in the 1920s were later photographed at a reunion *(left)*. Left to right, they are: Berry Brooks, Louis Furbinger, Gilbert Delugach, Fred Pritchard, Bill Heiskill, Charles Ward, Frank Miller, and Van Dresser. Some of the Eagle Scouts of 1930 *(below)* were, left to right, first row: Ed Spinks, Troop 11; Henrley Johnson, Troop 40; and Ira Archer, Troop 15. Second row: Robert Walls, Jr., Troop 11; Courtney Curl, Troop 10; and Dick Clarke, Troop 26. (CA)

DETECTIVES of the Memphis Police Department pose by a police touring car in front of police headquarters in the early 1930s. Benbow Clark is on the left, and the third man from the right, in the light coat, is Lee Quianty, Sr. Their riot guns are twelve-gauge, Winchester Model-97 pump shotguns. (Thompson)

THE TENNESSEE CLUB, during the early 1930s, when this picture was made, looked much as it had during the nineteenth century. Located at the northwest corner of Second and West Court, it is virtually unchanged today, although most of the buildings around it have been removed. (C of C)

COMPLETELY MECHANIZED and well trained, the Memphis Fire Department by 1930 was making progress toward its rating a few years later as one of the ten best in the nation. Firemen from Station Fifteen were, in front, left to right, A. Carpenter, E. Steadman, and F. Milazzo and his sons; the back row, left to right, are I. Sanders, F. Carpenter, J. Jones, and E. Thompson. The others are unidentified. (MPL)

BEALE STREET BLUES

"BEALE STREET...WHERE THE BLUES BEGAN"

SCENES REPRODUCED BY COURTESY OF THE COMMERCIAL APPEAL OF MEMPHIS, TENN., FROM THE DEDICATION OF HANDY SQUARE ON BEALE, MARCH 29, 1931.
UPPER LEFT—THE CROWD GATHERED IN SQUARE. UPPER RIGHT IN CAR LEADING PARADE—W. C. HANDY WITH LIEUT. G. W. LEE. LOWER LEFT—PARADE PASSING DOWN BEALE. LOWER RIGHT, SCHOOL CHILDREN IN FLOATS PASSING REVIEWING STAND. CITY, STATE AND FEDERAL OFFICIALS WERE AMONG THE LONG LIST OF SPEAKERS WHO WERE HEARD OVER RADIO AND CAUGHT BY MOVING PICTURE CAMERAS.

W. C. HANDY, Memphis' most famous musician before Elvis Presley, was honored by a parade on Beale Street on March 29, 1931. At the upper left of the photograph the crowd gathers in the square; at the upper right, the parade is led by an open car carrying W. C. Handy and Lt. George W. Lee, a Memphis insurance executive. The procession passes eastward on Beale Street (at lower left), and school children with floats pass by the reviewing stand (at lower right). Numerous city, state, and federal officials took this opportunity to pay tribute to the noted black musician, and to provide the crowd with their oratory. (MPL)

[114]

RICHARD HALLIBURTON, born in Memphis at the beginning of the twentieth century, lived a life of adventure that most people only dream of, and by writing about his adventures became one of the city's most widely read authors. Following his graduation from Princeton in 1921, he became a world traveler and adventurer, describing his experiences in his books: *Royal Road to Romance, New Worlds to Conquor, Glorious Adventure, The Flying Carpet,* and *Seven League Boots.* His exploits included crossing the Alps on an elephant, swimming the Hellespont, and circumnavigating the earth in a small biplane. He was lost at sea in 1939 while trying to cross the Pacific in a Chinese junk. Halliburton Memorial Tower, on the campus of Southwestern at Memphis, was later built in his honor. (CA)

CLARENCE SAUNDERS, who established the Piggly Wiggly grocery store chain, was one of the city's greatest business entrepreneurs of the twentieth century. Born in poverty in Virginia in 1881, he came to Memphis as a salesman for a grocery firm in 1904. Twelve years later he opened his first Piggly Wiggly store at 79 Jefferson. Using revolutionary methods of organization, marketing, and advertising, he soon expanded the chain until more than twelve hundred stores were in operation. In 1923, as a result of actions of the New York Stock Exchange, he went broke and lost Piggly Wiggly. He soon established another chain, "Clarence Saunders, Sole Owner of My Name Stores, Inc.," but this venture failed during the Depression. During the 1930s, the time of this photograph, he organized a new electrically powered grocery, Keedoozle, but it lasted only a few years. (MPL)

A FLOODLIGHT TRUCK, placed in service on February 7, 1935, was the newest addition to the Memphis Fire Department. Powered by a ten-kilowatt generator, it was equipped with five mounted lights and a dozen portable ones. This was a useful contribution to the department, since many fires in the city had always occurred at night. (MPL)

THE MOST MODERN AIR SERVICE in Memphis was represented by these Southern Airlines biplanes during the early 1930s. Paved runways were in use, but air traffic control was primitive by today's standards. (Thompson)

MADISON AVENUE is seen looking eastward from Front Street during the mid-1930s. Traffic is light, perhaps more from the early afternoon heat than from the economic effects of the Depression. The large structure at the right is the Exchange Building. (C of C)

THE MEDICAL SCHOOL of the University of Tennessee brought most of the physicians and dentists who practiced in the mid-South to Memphis for their training. The placing of the medical school at Memphis, at the other end of the state from the land-grant portion of the University of Tennessee at Knoxville, reflected the political realities of a long, narrow state at a time when transportation was slow and difficult. Opened windows in the building indicate that during the 1930s, when this photo was made, air-conditioning was not yet available. (C of C)

THE 1887-MODEL STEAM LOCOMOTIVE *(left)*, thirty feet long and weighing 72,000 pounds, was used by the Illinois Central Railroad until the 1930s. Illinois Central's major line ran from Chicago to New Orleans through Memphis. The newer model *(below)*, in service in the 1930s, was eighty-nine feet long and weighed 367,800 pounds. (CA)

THE FEDERAL BARGE LINE, which carried a large volume of the freight on the Mississippi, was one of the major businesses operating in Memphis in the early twentieth century. This view is of its River Rail Transfer Terminal where freight was interchanged between barges and trains. Between the two World Wars, when this photograph was made, steamboats were disappearing and most freight was carried by strings of barges pushed by diesel-powered boats like the one seen here at right corner. (MPL)

[117]

ROBERT CHURCH, SR.'s tradition of success was carried on by the other generations of his family. As active in political leadership as his father had been in business, Robert R. Church, Jr., became one of the most influential leaders of the Republican Party in the South. In 1917, he organized the NAACP in Memphis and Tennessee and was the first Southern member of its National Board of Directors. Republican national leaders sought his advice concerning appointments and policy in the South. He was a delegate to eight Republican National Conventions. Above, he is shown with Kansas Gov. Alfred Landon during Landon's campaign for the presidency in 1936. He was driven out of Memphis by the Crump political machine during Wendell Willkie's campaign in 1940. Roberta Church, his daughter, shown at right with Dwight Eisenhower during his first presidential campaign, inherited her father's aims and abilities, becoming the first black woman member of the Tennessee Republican Executive Committee. (RRC)

[118]

BLACK ELKS of Memphis gathered in 1937 outside of Church Auditorium to celebrate the re-activation of Bluff City Lodge No. 96 of the Improved Benevolent Protection Order of Elks of the World. The lodge had been organized about 1906 in the city, but white Elks who objected to the black lodge members wearing lapel pins similar to theirs, had secured a court injunction forbidding the black lodge from functioning in Tennessee. After thirty years of effort, Robert R. Church, Jr., succeeded in having the injunction lifted. He is seated at the front center wearing a white hat (see arrow). (RRC)

THE MEMPHIS COUNTRY CLUB featured an excellently landscaped eighteen-hole golf course during the 1930s, when this photograph of golfers enjoying an afternoon game was made. At this time, Buntyn Station on the Southern Railroad was still located south of the club. The building seen here was erected to replace an earlier structure which was destroyed in a fire in 1910. (C of C)

THE TITUS BLOCK, probably Memphis' first apartment house, was constructed after the Civil War when there was interest in the row house, a form of building used extensively in such cities as Baltimore and Philadelphia. Located on North Second near Market Square, it remained in use until after World War II. This photograph of its south and west elevations was made during the 1930s by Richard Bolton. (TSLA)

THE COTTON CARNIVAL, founded in 1931 by the city's businessmen, was intended to replace the Memphis Mardi Gras, which had been defunct since 1901. Formed to stimulate interest in Memphis business as well as to provide an occasion for celebration, the Cotton Carnival featured an arrival of the major participants by barge at the waterfront—as in this photo made in 1934 *(below)*—and a court of carnival royalty. Beauty was usually considered in the selection of the carnival queen *(above)*—an example of which is seen in this 1937 photo—while the king was traditionally a somewhat older man associated with the cotton industry or the cotton carnival. (MPL)

COLORFUL PARADES were a main feature of the Memphis Cotton Carnival every year. Black laborers were used to pull the floats during the early years. These photos were made during the carnival of 1937. (MPL)

IN THE BUSINESS DISTRICT, many Memphians still rode streetcars during the late 1930s. This view is from the east side of Main Street on a cloudy day shortly before World War II. (MATA)

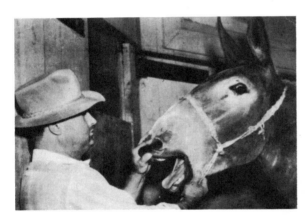

MULES have been a major economic asset to the city during most of its history. Tennessee mules have been famous throughout the nation; and most county seats in the state have had regularly scheduled dates, known as mule days, for the sale of these animals. Memphis remained the largest mule market in the world until the 1960s. This surprised-looking mule is having its teeth examined by ringman P. D. Carroll, a skilled professional whose estimates of mules' ages were noted for their accuracy. (MPL)

AMERICA'S MOST FAMOUS MULE AUCTIONEER, 368-pound Col. M. R. Meals, probably presided at the sale of more mules than any person in the nation. From his start in 1914, he estimated that he sold more than one million mules at Memphis auctions. This photograph was made around 1924. The best year for sales was 1918, when purchasing agents from the United States and European armies were buying Sales of these animals have declined since cotton plantations and coal mines, both major users of mules, have become mechanized. (MPL)

THIS EARLY FLYING BOAT being watched by a crowd of curious spectators during the flood of 1937 was one of the most efficient, if not safest, methods of travel around the area at that time. The view is west from the Memphis wharf toward the Arkansas shore. Only the tops of the trees on Mud Island are in sight above the water. (MPL)

THE MEMPHIS AIRPORT had regular flight schedules to most large American cities when this aerial photo was made on March 18, 1936. The major expansion of the field was to take place after World War II. (TSLA)

WALTER "FURRY" LEWIS, who was born at Greenwood, Mississippi, in 1893, came to Memphis at the age of six to begin a career that made him one of the city's internationally famous musicians. His reputation improved after W. C. Handy saw the boy playing on Beale Street, standing on a cigar box which he carried from place to place for his performances, and bought the young musician a good guitar. Furry has played at such diverse places as Pee Wee's Saloon on Beale Street, and Madison Square Garden and Carnegie Hall in New York. He also played in 1932 at the first Blues Festival in Philadelphia. (HEG)

"LITTLE LAURA" DUKES, for several decades one of Memphis' most popular blues singers, is the daughter of Alex Dukes, W. C. Handy's drummer. The musician at left is Huey Walker, who worked as a trombone player for Handy. Both Little Laura and Huey are still performing today. (HEG)

[124]

ONE OF THE GREAT BLUES MUSICIANS, Booker T. Washington "Bukka" White, was born in Aberdeen, Mississipi, in 1909, and moved to Memphis in 1930. His most famous song was "Aberdeen Blues." A pessimistic theme is characteristic of most of his songs, perhaps as a result of early experiences as a prisoner in the Mississippi State Penitentiary. He is still performing, although like many other Memphis musicians, he is better known nationally than in his own city. (HEG)

World War II and After

MEMPHIS RESIDENTS, like other Americans, had hardly recovered from the Great Depression before they were involved in the immense struggle of World War II. By the close of the 1930s the city had entered another period of growth and expansion, although more cautious and limited than that of the 1920s. With determined support in Washington, national agricultural prices had started improving.

As cotton's position bettered, the prospects for Memphis business also bettered. By 1940, the population had increased to 292,942, and continued to grow. Close political control of the city was being exercised by the Crump political machine, but the policies of Mr. Crump were generally considered favorable to business, and continued expansion of Memphis industry could reasonably have been expected. But the Japanese attack on Pearl Harbor on December 7, 1941, interrupted this placid trend—and the life of most residents of the city.

During the war almost everything was influenced by the full mobilization for the war effort. The Cotton Carnival was suspended, large numbers of men entered military service, and civilians took part in bond drives and other efforts to conserve materials needed for the war. The activities of many citizens were slowed by rationing and the restrictions of wartime travel. Reports from the battle areas became paramount, as Memphis families looked each day for news about members in the various armed forces. Men in uniform were common on the streets, and the Naval Station at Millington expanded for wartime training.

Residents of the city took a special pride in the exploits of the *Memphis Belle,* the B-17 heavy bomber that was returned to Memphis after successful operations in bombing raids over Germany. Business conditions remained prosperous, a result of intense government stimulation of the economy in order to secure maximum production for the U. S. war effort, and to send supplies to allied nations. The end of the war was a welcome event, though, with thousands of veterans returning to take part in a civilian economy that was expanding rapidly as consumer demand bounced prices upward.

After the war, a period of rapid growth started that was to double the population of the city during the next generation, marked in 1949 by the new Memphis-Arkansas Bridge across the Mississippi River which replaced the Harahan Bridge, now inadequate as a major artery for motor traffic.

The iron grip of the Crump machine began to lose some of its strength as the increasing size of the city made it more difficult to control. Mr. Crump's first major defeat was experienced in 1948 when a young Chattanooga lawyer, Estes Kefauver, was elected to the United States Senate despite Crump's opposition. The old political leader continued to dominate the city, however, until his death in 1954.

By that time, a new city was developing. The first Holiday Inn had been opened, new businesses were appearing in large numbers, and the Bluff City was quickly entering a new phase of expansion.

THE U.S.S. *Memphis,* a light cruiser of 7,050-tons displacement, was launched in 1924 as the fourth ship to bear the name of the city. This photo was made in 1939, after which the ship saw action in World War II before being taken out of service in 1945. (CA)

AN AERIAL VIEW of Memphis in 1940 shows Riverside Drive extending north from the lower right corner. Tom Lee Park between it and the River is not completed, and a large waterfront area is exposed by low water. Here, the Sterick Building is still the tallest on the city skyline. (MPL)

WOMEN DURING WORLD WAR II found new opportunities to work as the military service of large numbers of men created a labor shortage. The Memphis Street Railway Company employed these ladies to take surveys and to aid passengers. (MATA)

THE *MEMPHIS BELLE, (below)* a B-17 bomber with a distinguished combat record, was brought to the city and placed on display at the National Guard Armory in 1950. Although no member of the crew had lived in the city, its pilot was romantically involved with a Memphis girl, Margaret Polk *(right)*, and named the airplane for her. The *Belle* became the first B-17 to complete twenty-five missions over Europe and return to the United States under its own power. Damaged repeatedly in raids, the plane had to have seven new engines, two new wings, and a new tail section. The crew shot down eight enemy fighters, and earned a total of fifty-one decorations. (Polk)

RIVERSIDE DRIVE, seen looking north from Ashburn Park, served as a traffic artery to the downtown area in 1942, although the dogwood trees which decorate the bluff today had not yet been planted. Because of wartime needs, no new cars were being built at this time. The large building visible on the bluff is the Municipal Auditorium. (MPL)

THE MEMPHIS DOWNTOWN AREA featured parking meters and garages by the time of World War II, although traffic was limited because of wartime restrictions on driving. This view is south toward cotton row during a winter afternoon in the early 1940s. Gerber's Tea Room, located in the John Gerber Building (in the center of the photo, with the higher Falls Building behind it), was a favorite lunching place for workers in the business district and for women who then did their shopping downtown. (C of C)

UNION AVENUE is seen in this photograph looking west from the Commercial Appeal Building on a summer morning in 1942. Many men from the city were away at war, and only a few cars are on the street. The Peabody Hotel is at the left and the Sterick Building is still the tallest one in the city. (MPL)

A SPECTACULAR FIRE downtown was the one at the Court Avenue Garage on March 28, 1944, which brought a maximum response from the Memphis Fire Department. The department had the highest rating for efficiency and did prevent the spread of the fire, but the building was destroyed. (MPL)

THE MISSISSIPPI RIVER BANKS required unremitting attention, even after the completion of the levee system. These men, working on the left bank several miles below Memphis, are paving the banks, which have been graded and given a gravel covering. This type of protection prevented valuable land from washing away and stabilized the location of navigation channels. The photograph was made on June 25, 1945. (MPL)

SEVERAL INDIAN MOUNDS are located inside the Memphis city limits. This one, seen in a photograph made about the time of World War II, is the western mound in De Soto Park. Partly excavated on top, it was hollowed out during the Civil War by federal troops who used it for an artillery redoubt to cover the Mississippi River, which is located below the bluff on the opposite side of the mound. De Soto Park, like the newest bridge over the River at Memphis, is named for the Spanish explorer, Hernando de Soto, although the place where he actually reached the River had never been determined. (C of C)

[131]

PRESIDENT'S ISLAND, located in the Mississippi River below Memphis, had been an area for cotton planting until the 1950s. It provided several hundred acres of land near the city, but its industrial potential could not be developed until the east channel around the island, the Tennessee Chute, could be closed. This photograph, made by the U. S. Army Corps of Engineers on May 16, 1951, shows the building of the Jack Carley Causeway, connecting the island with the Tennessee shore. The closure dam is almost completed, but the paving has not yet been done. (MPL)

THE END OF THE LINE for streetcars of the Memphis Street Railway Company in the early 1940s was at Pendleton on Lamar Avenue. Under summertime cumulus clouds, this bus is turning to start its journey back to the downtown area. (MATA)

[132] ARKANSAS AND OLE MISS met often in Memphis for football clashes. Since Memphis was situated on the boundary of each of the states, neither of which had a city comparably large, it was the perfect setting for both Rebel and Razorback fans. A football weekend in Memphis was characterized by parties, shopping, and revelry. In this photo, made in the late 1940s on a fall afternoon in Crump Stadium, the score is 0 to 0. The Ole Miss-Arkansas schedule has now been suspended, and major games are played in the new stadium at the fairgrounds, Liberty Bowl Memorial Stadium. The building in center background is Central High School. (MSU)

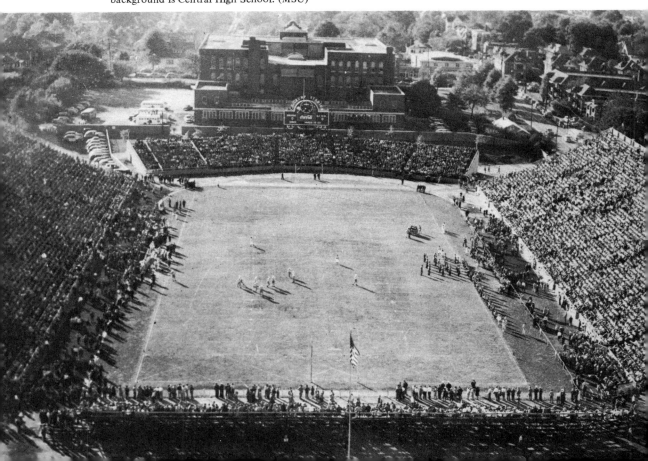

MEMPHIS STATE COLLEGE's basketball team poses with Coach Zack Curlin in the old College Field House during the 1945 season. Memphis State's greatest success in basketball lay more than a decade in the future, after it would receive university status in 1957. (MSU)

MEMPHIS' MISS AMERICA was Barbara Jo Walker, selected at Atlantic City in 1947. At that time a Memphis State College student, she refused Hollywood offers and was married the following year to Dr. John Hummel. This photo was made of her while modeling during one of her tours as Miss America. (CA)

[133]

THE CENSOR OF MEMPHIS was Lloyd T. Binford, who for more than a quarter of a century decided which movies residents of the city could see. Born in 1866 at Duck Hill, Mississippi, he had little formal schooling, but displayed an early talent in business. After his first success as a teenager, when he cornered the firecracker market in Duck Hill, he engaged in other successful ventures until he organized the Columbian Mutual Life Insurance Company, and in 1921 moved its headquarters to Memphis. Seven years later he had become the censor of the city, where he won attention by banning a succession of movies. He was incensed with Charlie Chaplin, whom he considered a "London guttersnipe," and with Ingrid Bergman, whose personal life did not meet his approval; he also objected to movies displaying blacks and whites doing things he disapproved of, such as attending school together. He also banned some movies with themes dealing with sexual or criminal activity. Known as the "Sporting Deacon," he was a Baptist deacon who raised thorough-bred horses on his Mississippi plantation. (CA)

BANNED IN MEMPHIS was the fate of the statuesque actress Jane Russell in her movie *The Outlaw* in 1946. This photo was made of her while filming *Son of Paleface,* in which she starred also. (CA)

PEE WEE'S SALOON, at 317 Beale Street *(below),* was the most popular hangout of Memphis musicians during the W. C. Handy era. It was here that Handy worked on "St. Louis Blues" and "Memphis Blues." This photograph was made in the 1930s after the saloon had closed and a dry-cleaning shop occupied the building. The "Jug" bands carried on the tradition of Beale Street jazz. A session in Handy Park *(right)* includes several well-known musicians: The woman in black near the left is "Ma Rainey," still living today, who in her youth had performed with the original Ma Rainey. The man with his foot on the tub is Dewey Corley, who recorded under his own name and several others before his death in the 1970s. He also played with the Beale Street Sheiks. The man in the right foreground is "Washboard Sam." (HEG)

THE FLOATS of the Cotton Carnival parades became more elaborate after World War II, and they were motorized rather than hand-pulled. Agriculture *(above)* and Indian heritage *(right)* were represented by these beautiful floats, while the one below seems to resemble a boat. (TSLA)

MEMPHIS' LIFELINES during the twentieth century came to be its roads, as motor transport supplanted steamboats and trains. Ironically, the River, which had been the city's major avenue in flatboat and steamboat days, was only a barrier to cars and trucks, and it became necessary to build a new span to replace the inadequate Harahan Bridge. Also, a fire in 1928 that had destroyed the old bridge's roadways demonstrated the risk of depending on a partly wooden structure. Much of the material for the new bridge would be barged to the site. During 1949, residents of the city watched the completion of the new Memphis-Arkansas Bridge *(below)*. The photo *(above, left)* of workers moving like human flies along the beams was made in September, and the picture of the connecting of the remaining girders *(above, right)* was made later. The three ironworkers are Jack Nelson, Ted Crawford, and Hubert Spradling. Ted Crawford is still working as a foreman of ironworkers today—twenty-six years later. (CA)

[136]

THE FIRST HOLIDAY INN, opened on Summer Avenue on August 1, 1952, was the beginning of a major international business headquartered in Memphis. Founded by Kemmons Wilson, a home builder, the motel chain grew rapidly after another builder, Wallace Johnson, joined the partnership a few years later. There are now about 3,000 Holiday Inns in the United States and other nations. This first motel was retired by Holiday Inns in 1973, and is now the Royal Oaks Motel. (Bobbitt)

BOSS OF A POLITICAL MACHINE powerful enough to choose all office holders in Memphis, E. H. Crump was also able to select governors of the state. He was able to give almost the entire vote of Shelby County, the largest in Tennessee, to the candidate of his choice. This portrait was made late in life, after his red hair had turned white. (CL)

THE OLD AND NEW in Tennessee politics appeared together in Memphis at a benefit football game in behalf of the blind on December 4, 1953. E. H. Crump had less than a year left to live at this date, but Frank Clement's political career was just beginning. He had been inaugurated governor that year after being elected with Boss Crump's support. (CA)

VISITING WITH FRIENDS was one of Mr. Crump's greatest pleasures. He enjoyed horse racing at Hot Springs, the Cotton Carnival in Memphis, and various other activities. This photograph, made in 1951, is of (left to right in the box) Mrs. L. W. Hughes, Walter Chandler, Mrs. Eugene Bearman, E. H. Crump, and Mrs. C. Frank Scott. (CA)

POWER IN MEMPHIS was held by a small number of men during the Crump era. This informal photo is of Cliff Davis, Walter Chandler, E. H. Crump, and E. W. Hale. (CA)

A POLITICAL LEADER who rose to prominence in the Crump era and survived the transition period through the 1950s was Clifford Davis. Working his way up through municipal offices in the political machine after his graduation from law school at the University of Mississippi, he became the congressman from Memphis. He is shown here with Mrs. Davis and a young Tennesseean with a brilliant, though brief, political career ahead of him—Frank Clement. (MPL)

W. C. HANDY was Memphis' most famous musician until Elvis Presley became an internationally known performer in the late 1950s. This photograph made about 1940, of Handy reading *(right)* was his wife's favorite. Blind, but still a master with the trumpet, Handy returned to Memphis near the end of his life. The photograph *(above)* was probably made in 1955 when he was helping raise money for his statue in Handy Park. His fame continued to increase after his death. The original Preservation Hall Band of New Orleans came to Memphis for the beginning of the Memphis Cotton Carnival Annual Jazz Festival. They are shown here below saluting the Handy statue on Beale Street. (HEG)

NO OTHER MEMPHIAN has ever achieved as much international recognition as rock-and-roll singer Elvis Presley, who was born January 8, 1935, in Mississippi, and moved to the city during mid-1947. After graduating from Humes High School in 1952, he worked briefly as a truck driver for Sun Electric Corporation, but by 1953 he had started his career and was singing in Overton Park and elsewhere. The portrait at left was made during this time. Presley, who had seven dollars left after paying his bills one day, went to the Fox Studio on Madison Avenue, where he ordered the photograph. Fame came rapidly thereafter. Within the next few years he became one of the most successful singers in the nation, as the audience for his records and movies continued to increase. Below, Elvis' parents, Mr. and Mrs. Vernon Presley of Memphis, visit him in 1957 while he is working on the set of Paramount's *Loving You.* During a recording session for the movie *Jailhouse Rock,* he is seen *(above)* with the Jordanaires—Neal Mathews at the left, Hoyt Hawkins at the piano, Hugh Jarrett at the right, and Gordon Stoker in the right background. Scotty Moore is playing the guitar. Hometown friends are Arthur Wooten at the extreme left, and George Klein, in the left background. Klein is a well-known radio personality in Memphis today. (Dredge)

Index